POOR
LITTLE
RICH
SLUM

what we saw in Dharavi and why it matters

POOR LITTLE RICH SLUM

Rashmi Bansal
Deepak Gandhi

Photos by Dee Gandhi

westland

westland ltd
Venkat Towers, 165, P.H. Road, Maduravoyal, Chennai 600 095
No. 38/10 (New No.5), Raghava Nagar, New Timber Yard Layout, Bangalore 560 026
Survey No. A - 9, II Floor, Moula Ali Industrial Area, Moula Ali, Hyderabad 500 040
23/181, Anand Nagar, Nehru Road, Santacruz East, Mumbai 400 055
4322/3, Ansari Road, Daryaganj, New Delhi 110 002

First published by westland ltd 2012

10 9 8 7 6 5 4 3 2 1

ISBN: 978-93-81626-18-4

Typeset by Magic Touch

Printed at Manipal Technologies Ltd., Manipal

Dedicated to
Sadhguru Jaggi Vasudev
of Isha Foundation

Because what lies *within* is what really matters

AUTHORS' NOTE

I have lived in Mumbai most of my life but never set foot inside Dharavi.

Not until 15 February 2011, when we made our first, tentative trip to explore the idea of this book.

Deepak strongly felt this book needed to be written, I was not so sure.

Who wants to read about slums? Only professors of sociology and NGO-types.

But maybe, that's why this book *had* to be written.

We are ordinary middle-class citizens.
The kind who employ maids and drivers from slums.

We are 'decent' human beings.
The kind who think mainly about our own comforts and careers.

We didn't go into Dharavi with an overactive conscience. We went there with a sense of adventure. To discover, what the *hell* this place is all about.

In the beginning, it was difficult. We could not see beyond the obvious – the garbage, the filth, the 'sluminess' of the slum.

One afternoon, straight from Dharavi, we went to have lunch at the Trident Hotel in BKC, just two kilometres away. The toilet cubicle was bigger than the house we'd just visited.

Pasta didn't slide down our throats that afternoon.
The unfairness of it all, suddenly came alive.

Over time, we grew familiar with people and places in Dharavi. We looked into the eyes of a civilisation, and saw beauty within the chaos.

This book is an attempt to share that expansive experience, through the limited medium of words and pictures. Writing it restored our faith in humanity. We can be happy, we can be hopeful, we can be enterprising – no matter where we are.

The question is – are you?

If Dharavi can, so can I.

January 2012, Mumbai   Rashmi Bansal, Deepak Gandhi, Dee Gandhi

SECTION 1

DHARAVI, WHAT EES?

We wish they would not exist, but we cannot wish them away. Sixty per cent of our city is a slum and it all started here, in Dharavi.

CHAPTER 1

A
BLOODY
BIG FAT
PROBLEM

"What's the big deal anyway?"

It was six men of Indostan
To learning much inclined,
Who went to see the Elephant
(Though all of them were blind),
That each by observation
Might satisfy his mind...

And so these men of Indostan
Disputed loud and long,
Each in his own opinion
Exceeding stiff and strong,
Though each was partly in the right,
And all were in the wrong!

– John Godfrey Saxe

Dharavi is an elephant of an issue with blind men scrambling all over it. Each sees a small part of the picture and considers it to be the 'whole'.

To the residents of Dharavi, it is a way of life. They live here, work here, marry here and even die here. What's the big deal anyway?

"Bombay mein sab log aisaich rehte hain, idhar family hai, biradari hai... yehi hamara ghar hai."

The resident of Dharavi is blind to the inconvenience of living in a place where one toilet is shared by 1,440 residents. Because he knows no other world.

To the residents of high-rise buildings in Mumbai – a small but important slice of people – Dharavi is 'Asia's largest slum'. A filthy place you see through a car, with windows rolled up tight.

Silently admiring the leather bags in the boutiques on Sion-Dharavi Link Road. Mentally noting, "I must stop here some time!"

The high-rise resident is blind to the community and kinship of Dharavi. To the little girl who may live in a 100 sq ft house with eight other siblings, but still has a smile in her eyes.

To the businessmen who operate in Dharavi, it is a convenience. Cheap labour and cheap rent make it a mega-hub of micro-enterprise. $650 million is the sum total of Dharavi's annual turnover.

"Idhar sab tarah ka kaam hota hai!"

The businessman is blind to the toll on human life. The living conditions, the working conditions, leave much to be desired. But as long as *dhandha chal raha hai*, who cares?

To the builder who proposes to redevelop Dharavi, it is a goldmine. 1.7 sq km in the heart of the city, right next to the upmarket Bandra Kurla Complex.

"You see, Dharavi is value waiting to be unlocked."

The builder is blind to the human beings who 'occupy' this prime property. All he can see are the zeros people will pay for fancy new apartments. If only those pesky residents could somehow be persuaded to move, into a 225 sq ft 'free house'.

To the government, who 'owns' Dharavi, it is a time-bomb. Redevelopment will bring in much-needed money into state coffers. But how much of it will come into our pockets, is what they really want to know.

"We promise to make Mumbai into Shanghai," they say.

The government is blind to its responsibility. It is their duty to create a safe, clean and well-functioning environment. Not an 'option', a measure in hindsight.

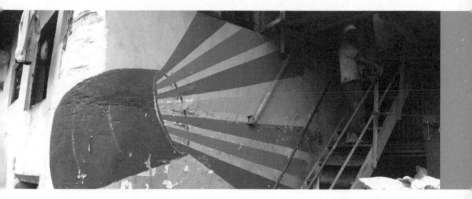

To the outsiders who come to Dharavi, it is a project. Filmmakers, artists, poets and PhD students are all flocking there to 'study' the slum experience.

"We get to learn so many new things here, understand a different way of life!"

The outsider is blind to the drudgery of Dharavi. He chooses to see a colourful, chaotic, creatively inspirational mess. We watch these blind men as they scramble over the elephant of Dharavi. It is an amusing sight and, at the same time, a tragic one.

POOR
LITTLE
RICH
SLUM

CHAPTER 2

SCRAMBLING OVER THE ELEPHANT

"In Dharavi everyone is too
busy doing their own thing..."

When I first heard about 'Dharavi Slum Tours' a couple of years ago, I thought to myself, "Ugh".

Is it right to parade 'poverty' as just another tourist attraction Mumbai has to offer? Riding on the wave created by *Slumdog Millionaire*?

And yet, here we were, at Mahim Station. Armed with sunglasses, caps and water bottles, waiting for our 'tour guide'.

A young man with a casual gait and a shy smile walks up to us.

"Hello, I am Tauseef...you spoke to me yesterday," he says.

We follow him, climb up a bridge across the railway tracks, and begin the 'tour'.

"This is the commercial side of Dharavi," he explains, as we stop outside a large, cavernous godown of sorts. Inside is a 30 ft high pile of assorted garbage. Half a dozen men and women are sitting in there, separating plastic, metal and paper.

There is no fan, or natural ventilation and it is hot, very hot. But the workers seem to be okay with it. A bored-looking middle-aged man sits nearby, sharing the heat and dust, keeping a semi-vigilant eye.

Abu* has been in this business for the last thirty years.

"My family still lives in the village," he says. "But soon my elder son may join me here."

We move on, past a unit melting down plastic scrap into pellets. The smoke this produces is noxious, black and certainly not good for health. But all's fair in love, war and business.

"Are all these units registered?" I ask Tauseef.

"Not all...but this one is," he points to a unit making corrugated boxes. It looks more organised, professional, with some heavy machinery.

Not very typical of Dharavi.

Our next stop is a one-room unit making pipes – all shapes, sizes and circumference. On the grey façade of the drab building is a colourful red and blue mural bearing the legend 'Pipe Wallah'.

"That was a group of foreigners who came here and did some art workshops," explains Tauseef. "They painted the walls also."

We peek into more small businesses – people making brooms, sharpening blades, running a laundry. No one seems to care about us tourists, craning our necks into their workspace, asking somewhat intrusive questions.

Tauseef shrugs. "In Dharavi, everyone is too busy doing their own thing..."

Even tourism is yet another business.

We leave the 13th Compound, cross a sludgy green and stinky *nullah*, to the residential side of Dharavi. But here too, enterprise is everywhere.

A bakery is cranking out *khari* biscuits in an old-fashioned coal-fired oven. A worker dressed in *banian* and *lungi* expertly shovels the dough inside. Retrieving the puffs a few minutes later, perfectly crisped and golden brown.

The owner is sitting there, brown and swarthy, pride evident in his voice.

"We supply to all the Irani restaurants of Bombay...our product is best so we have high demand. Here, taste one!"

A little further down, a group of teenagers sits huddled, assembling suitcases. The piece we pick up bears the legend 'Cleartrip' – probably inspired by the popular travel website.

"*Yahan kab se ho?*" we ask the boys.

They are all recent immigrants to the city, from Bihar. And they are neither pleased nor displeased with their lot. This is life; to live you have to work. Dharavi has work, and that is good enough, for now.

It is the same at the *zari*-embroidery unit. To reach it, we climb up a 20 ft high iron ladder. Here, on the 'first floor', sit young boys, no more than 13 or 14. Along with a middle-aged balding man.

Their job is to fix sequins onto bright red cloth. With flying fingers, they create intricate silver petals, leaves and swirls. Not at all as effortless as it seems...

"*Main yahan pandrah saal se hoon,*" says the balding man. The others are recent arrivals; he is teaching them the craft.

The room is relatively airy and sunlit, the ceiling high. Clothes hang on pegs in the corners, a fourteen-inch TV sits against one wall.

"We work here, we eat here, we live here," he explains. "This is all and everything to us."

The high point of our tour is the view from the roof of the zari unit.

"Be careful," says Tauseef. For we might step on shredded plastic waste, spread all over the floor to dry in the sun.

Corrugated tin roofs spread out as far as the eye can see. Some taller than others, a few bearing satellite dishes. We are not builders or town planners, but even we can sense that this is a *lot* of land.

Land that can be freed up if the area is redeveloped into multistoreyed buildings. Creating space for gardens, schools with playgrounds, and modern industrial estates.

Why then, are people willing to live like this?

Yes, Dharavi is a cauldron bubbling with enterprise, with a never-say-die attitude. With spirit and spunk. But all is not well. Tauseef leads us through the alleyways where people live, wall to wall, roof to roof.

Ten by ten feet rooms occupied by eight-member families, with barely enough space to stretch their legs. Stove in one corner, TV in another.

"If you are lucky, you have a loft," says Tauseef. A small area inside the house where you can climb up and sleep, or work.

But even that is surely not enough.... Where do people relax? How do children study? When do couples make love?

We can't ask these questions because they are stupid. Life is thriving here, obviously people somehow adjust.

They adjust to lack of privacy.

They adjust to lack of hygiene.

They adjust to lack of progress.

Because this is the only life they know. Dimly, they do know that there is something more, something better out there.

But what if I reach out for that dream and find that even what I have has slipped through my fingers?

At the end of the tour we are left wondering, is less really more?

* Name changed on request.

POOR
LITTLE
RICH
SLUM

CHAPTER 3

LESS
IS
MORE

POOR
LITTLE
RICH
SLUM

"What's the point of coming
to school?"

Less is evidently more at the Dharavi Transit Camp Municipal School.
There is a large playground, a well-constructed concrete building. But
Classroom 3 B is bare and sparsely furnished.

Tiny chairs with peeling paint are arranged against three walls. Where
are the tables?

"Uh, it seems there is no budget for tables. But we manage."

Kids sit on the floor and do their writing exercises.

"It was a shock when I first came here," admits Srini. He is one of the four young instructors at the school from 'Teach for India'. A programme inspired by 'Teach for America' which enables young professionals and graduates from India's elite colleges to 'give back'. By working for two years at a government or municipal school.

Srini Swaminathan is an engineer from the prestigious BITS Pilani. He got placed from campus with oil major Schlumberger – a job that made him the envy of his classmates.

"I spent eight years travelling across the world – Africa, South America, Middle East...and, of course, earned a lot of money."

Money which he donated online to various causes, but somehow that was not enough.

"I too come from a very poor family and I realised, I want to do something for kids who are in that situation. Struggling as I was those days."

Srini applied to 'Teach for India' and got selected. Trading in a dollar salary for a ₹ 15,000 stipend and a huge challenge.

"I had no idea how, or what I would be doing!"

The very first day he came to school, a well-wisher laid out the facts of life.

"Don't bother teaching in English."

"But isn't this an English-medium school?" asked Srini, surprised.

"*Haan*...but no one teaches in English. It's no use; they don't want to learn anyway."

Srini was shocked and amused and roused to action.

"These are just kids – 7 or 8 years old. Who says they don't want to learn?"

Srini decided the one thing that *had* to be taught was English. It could be their passport to a better world. But, of course, a mere A-B-C-D approach would not do.

Most of the kids – at age seven – did not know even that.

"Basically I had to make learning fun. I had to make it easy..."

To do that, Srini had to get creative. He devised a moving blackboard – an apron he wears so that kids can write on it with a marker.

"I go to them instead of them coming up to the board. They love it!"

More than writing or reading, Srini put the emphasis on conversation. He mandated that kids speak only in English in the class. To get them motivated to do so, he has a system of rewards.

"I put in a little money into a box every time a kid uses a new word. When the box is full, we have a little party for the whole class.

There's also a system of 'marbles' – a currency that little boys revere even more than cash.

With love and effort and perseverance, Srini says his class has picked up in all areas. And English, most of all.

"It used to be 90% Hindi, 10% English – now my kids speak 70% of the time in English."

And along with skills and motivation, Srini has also been working on aspirations. Answering the fundamental question – what's the point of coming to school?

"When I first asked the kids, 'What is your dream? *Bade hokar kya banna chahte ho?'* I got very basic responses."

Someone wanted to be a tea-stall owner. Work in a factory, or become a driver.

"Not one child said things like doctor, or engineer, or bank officer."

This, says Srini, is one of the basic differences between his low-income childhood, and Dharavi.

"I was always aware of the importance of education, encouraged at home to study and achieve something in life. Even though I was in a government school."

In Dharavi Transit Camp, if you are a girl, you will most likely drop out after Class 6 or 7. You will then be at home, helping your mother look after the house and younger siblings.

If you are a boy, you still have to be very motivated, as the school offers classes only till Class 7. To study further, you will have to shift elsewhere.

"You see, according to the Constitution, children have to be in school till age fourteen. So municipal schools – which provide free schooling – don't offer classes for older kids."

We've all heard of maidservants who spend a large chunk of their income to send their kids to a private school. To give them a better chance in life.

"Funnily enough, we have students here whose fathers are quite well-to-do – running a good business – but they still don't want to spend on education."

If the son has to join the business and the daughter is not meant to study beyond middle school – why bother?

"They really have no role models.... A large majority don't step out of Dharavi. They live here, work here, get everything they need here."

Whereas, the maidservant spends her days in middle-class homes.

"More than the fathers, the mothers have hopes for their kids, but they are helpless. We are illiterate, or can barely read and write – what can we do for the kids?"

When he visits homes, Srini tries to educate mothers on how everything is learning. Counting peas is an exercise, telling stories stimulates young minds.

"But with 6-7 children to look after, the mothers can only do so much."

Apart from housework, women spend a lot of their time fetching water. And, of course, wake up really, really early, in order to use public toilets, or find a place in the open to defecate.

"I think the women – who are stuck at home all day – have to cope with many more problems. They are very keen to see a better life, to have amenities in their homes."

The men can always escape to their place of work. Sit in a tea shop, or barber shop.

Drink, gamble or watch blue films in one of the many 'theatres' that dot Dharavi.

And, occasionally, give vent to frustration by beating their wives.

Still, Srini finds the overall atmosphere at Dharavi to be positive.

"I walk through muck and stench to reach the homes of my students.... The conditions they live in are appalling. Still, they will be smiling...they will be happy with the gift of a balloon."

The little iron ladder resting against every hut is what Srini sees as a symbol of Dharavi.

"That ladder is 'moving up in life'. If you have that extra space, to use for your work, or to rent out, you seem to have arrived in Dharavi."

Less is more once again. Less of everything, not just external things, physical things, but deep within.

And it is perhaps a good thing for the rest of us, the affluent class of this city. If, like Oliver Twist, the people of Dharavi decided to unite and ask for 'more' – would we be able to stand up to their might?

Lucky for us, they are relatively content, and willing to struggle within the system. Not stepping onto the streets, demanding a revolution.

Unlike the bandana-clad, gun-toting Naxalites, in Jharkhand and Bihar.

In Pali Hill, when a slum child comes out of his home, those rich people in their big cars look at him like he is a piece of dirt.

But here in Dharavi, everywhere, wherever we look, there are people like us. A child who grows up in Dharavi may be poor but he does not feel inferior.

That is why nobody can crush us, bulldoze us, wipe us out just like that.

– Raju Korde
Lawyer and social activist

CHAPTER 4

TALKIN' 'BOUT
A
REVOLUTION

POOR
LITTLE
RICH
SLUM

"We don't want to move
somewhere else."

Don't you know
They're talkin' 'bout a revolution
It sounds like a whisper...

While they're standing in the welfare lines
Crying at the doorsteps of those armies of salvation
Wasting time in the unemployment lines
Sitting around waiting for a promotion...

– Tracy Chapman
Talkin' 'bout a Revolution

There are many kinds of revolutions.

There's one kind where people carry flags and shout slogans, demanding their rights.

There's another, where people carry guns and shout slogans, seizing their rights.

But there's another, more subtle, form of revolution. You won't see flags, or guns, or collective chanting. Because this is a silent revolution, an individual revolution, where each man is striving to better his life.

That is the revolution you see in Dharavi. A revolution of energy and enterprise.

It started with the first arrivals in Dharavi – migrants from Tamil Nadu and Gujarat. They were mostly artisans, people who worked with their hands.

The Gujaratis were from Saurashtra, and they set up Kumbharwada – where they made pots.

The Maharashtrians of the Charmarkar caste also came to Dharavi, sowing the seeds for the leather industry.

Muslims from Tamil Nadu and UP used the skills they had, to set up tanneries.

Oddly enough, it was the wide-open space in Dharavi which attracted these people. And allowed such industries to flourish.

"*Jab mere dada yahan aye the, idhar kuch bhi nahin tha…*" is a constant refrain.

Dharavi was a no-man's land, considered to be outside the city. And, hence, it was the place which outsiders made their own.

There was no sign to greet the tired, the poor huddled masses coming in search of work to the city. But everyone knew.

You can come to Mumbai from anywhere in India and quickly find some work.

You can come to Dharavi from anywhere in India and quickly find some work, and a roof over your head.

This is as true today, as it was fifty years ago. Only, there are no wide-open spaces. In fact, there is no space at all.

"Yahan sab kuch hai – paisa achha hai, log achhe hain, par aasmaan nahin hai, jaan hai, jahan nahi hai."

Women, confined to their sunless tenements, suffer from osteoporosis.

Children have no slides or swings.

And yet, the fire of commerce and the fuel of hope keep Dharavi from reaching boiling point. The *bhattis* of discontent are too busy boiling colour to dye fabric.

The fists which could be in the air are busy stitching leather goods for fancy shops.

They may grumble about the conditions here, but one thing they are sure of.

"We don't want to move somewhere else."

There is an emotional attachment to this land, to this chaotic existence. You can take a man out of Dharavi, they say, but you cannot take Dharavi out of a man.

And that is why so many who move up and move out stay connected. They may check out, but in some sense, they can never leave…

POOR
LITTLE
RICH
SLUM

CHAPTER 5

US
VS
THEM

POOR
LITTLE
RICH
SLUM

"I have seen slums where people have LCD TV."

For a moment, forget that you are reading a book and put on your participation cap. Come, join us in this simple exercise: 'Choose the Worthiest Cause.'

You have ₹ 100 to donate to one of the following three causes. You must donate the entire amount to the cause of your choice.

Cause 1
Darfur, Sudan – a pressing humanitarian problem:
About three million people, including one million children, have been forced to abandon their homes due to civil war, resulting in massive food

shortage. In the last one week, 8,000 people, including 2,800 children, have died due to starvation. World citizens are earnestly requested to donate generously to save lives in Darfur.

Cause 2

Helping a girl-child get an education:

Rakhee (age nine) and Sultana (age eleven) are from a poor family and work as domestic help in one of the metro cities of India. There are thousands of girls like Rakhee and Sultana, who need a small financial gift from you to transform their lives. With your donation, they will be able to attend vocational school and secure sufficient skills to lead a decent and respectable life.

Cause 3

Improving slum conditions:

1,20,000 people are living in a slum in the heart of a city. Most of them are self-employed and somehow earn just enough to survive. Each family consists of eight members living in a 148 sq ft area. There is just one toilet for 350 families. Women and children have to collect water from one municipal tap, either early morning or late evening. With your donation, our NGO can help them build toilets and commission more taps to ease the problem.

Now close your eyes and listen to your heart. Who deserves your ₹ 100? Ask yourself, which cause touches you most deeply…

Did you decide to donate your money to save a starving child in Sudan? Well, then you think like the majority.

We posed the same question to 210 students from Wilson College and Jamnalal Bajaj Institute of Management Studies, and sixty-five per cent of them chose to donate to save a child from hunger.

"I am so sad to see the photos of hungry children, it is too shocking," wrote one student.

"It is the greatest tragedy of the twenty-first century," said another.

The immediacy of the situation is evident. Your actions can save a human life, even if it is in a distant location you had never heard of. You *want* to help.

Wait a minute, some of you are saying, that's not the cause you chose. Okay. We are pretty sure then you would have chosen Option 2 – education for the girl-child.

Twenty-nine per cent of the students we polled decided to use their money to help Rakhee and Sultana.

"Education is empowerment," declared one student.

"If a woman is educated, she will educate her children and uplift the entire family," said another.

The impact of your action is evident. Your donation can create a better life, a brighter future. You *want* to help.

If you chose Option 3, you are among a tiny minority in urban upper-class India. Barely six per cent of the two-hundred-odd students wished to donate to the cause of improving slum conditions.

"If slum conditions are improved, then the mindsets of slum dwellers will change and they will try to improve themselves," observed one student.

"Health and hygiene is a basic necessity of life, hence I choose this cause," said another.

The enormity of the situation is evident. Your action is helpful, but not heroic. Besides, you don't really *want* to help.

"The government is giving free houses to slum dwellers, but they sell the houses and move back into slums," said one agitated young man.

"I have seen slums where people have LCD TVs and Italian marble flooring," pointed out a second.

A lone voice of dissent in the classroom, a young man wearing a green T-shirt with the 'Peace' symbol.

"We have to accept slums…the plans to remove them won't work because there are too many poor people coming to Mumbai in search of jobs…. Where will they stay?"

If only we had asked this question fifty years ago…instead of leaving all these people to create their own solution. In tin and toil, and extreme toilet conditions.

To create a life, all on their own.

> "Politicians promise many things but forget after elections. So we have to be self-sufficient.
>
> We formed our own mandal – Ekvira Mitra Mandal – and constructed a pucca toilet block. 226 families of our area use this toilet and they pay just ₹ 20 per month. See how clean it is – we maintain it ourselves."
>
> – Dilip Gadekar
> Founder, Ekvira Mitra Mandal, Dharavi

POOR
LITTLE
RICH
SLUM

SECTION 2

THE INCUBATOR

In other slums, people go to work; here, they come looking for work. This is the spirit of human enterprise, in its natural form – raw and extreme.

CHAPTER 6

FACTORY
OF
DREAMS

"I never knew English…now
I have my own Facebook page."

Every room in Dharavi is 10 x 10. But this, is like no other. No crush of humanity, no pots and pans, no spices hanging heavy in the air.

The room is almost spacious, since it is so bare.

There are shiny, cream Marbonite tiles on the floor. A tiny refrigerator and a drum of water in one corner. And a washroom right next to it.

"Only for bath," explains Jameel, as we stare in amazement. "I can't build a toilet, unfortunately."

Jameel is what you can call a genuine Dharavi 'success story'. Unlike so many we met in Dharavi, it wasn't his grandfather or great-grandfather who settled here when it was marshland.

Jameel Shah came to Dharavi from a small village in Bihar, in the year 1995. Like any young boy from Bihar, he became a *kaarigar* at a workshop, for a salary of ₹ 2,000.

Fifteen short years later, he is running his own workshop. And not just any workshop. Jameel Shah makes 'dancing shoes' for the most exquisite feet in the country.

"See," he says, holding up a beautiful pair of blue satin heels, "this is for Bipasha Basu."

Bollywood stars like Katrina Kaif, Priyanka Chopra and Hrithik Roshan are among his 'regular clients'.

The story of Jameel Shah itself, could be made into a Bollywood film.

Born in a village in Bihar's Darbhanga district, Jameel is the oldest among four brothers and four sisters. His father was a landless labourer earning barely enough for two meals a day.

Jameel attended a madrasa run by the local mosque. One morning, he asked for money to buy a pen and notebook. There was none to spare.

In a fit of anger, he screamed at his father, *"Mera haq banta hai ki main padoon."*

And in that anger, Jameel ran away from home with a friend. He was ten years old.

He landed up in Delhi and worked at Navi Kareem, an area near Paharganj, housing hundreds of small workshops. Similar to Dharavi.

"I started making wallets and bags," recalls Jameel.

But it was not enough for him.

"I had seen so many films, I thought *bade log* all live in Bombay. I thought, to make money and make it big, I must also go to Bombay."

Thus, Jameel Shah arrived in Mumbai with a distant uncle. Initially, he worked in Bhiwandi, at a power loom. But the work was not to his liking.

"I had to stand and work there for 10-12 hours every day," says Jameel. "So I left it and came to Dharavi."

Through the village network, he located some boys to share a room with, and also got a job. Working in a leather factory by day, on nights and weekends, Jameel Shah started a small side business.

"Mobile covers were becoming popular, so I started selling them at VT and Manish Market."

Thanks to his extra income, Jameel managed to save ₹ 25,000. But, he lent the money to the brother of a friend, not knowing the fellow was a rascal.

One fine day, Jameel realised his life's savings were gone. He borrowed ₹ 1,000 from his *seth* to pursue the cheat and recover his cash. But when he reached Bangalore, the man had fled to Delhi.

"I did not even have money to eat," says Jameel. "I tried to get a job in a socks factory, but they said I need *pehchaan*."

It was a Bihari watchman at the Broadway Hotel who helped Jameel get some work. And, another accident of fate brought him into the home of 'Thomas Aunty'.

An old lady living alone in a bungalow, who needed help with odd-jobs at home.

"Aunty became so fond of me, she said, 'Stay here with me. I will look after you. Treat you like my own son'. "

But Jameel refused.

He said, "*Aap dua karo ki main achha karoon; wohi bahut hai mere liye.*"

One important thing happened in Bangalore. A man named Jacob who rented the room above Aunty's garage took him to a salsa dancing class.

"I danced and I learnt something new. I wanted to learn more, but I did not have money."

Eventually, Jameel returned to Mumbai, to his old employer in Dharavi. But the 'dancing bug' remained in his head.

He looked up advertisements in *Mid Day* and went searching for a class to join. That's how he met Sandip Soparrkar.

"First time I met Sandip sir, I said, 'I really want to learn dance, but I cannot give the full fees right now. Can I pay you little by little?' "

Sandip agreed.

Jameel not only learnt dancing, but also started helping with shows.

One thing every dancer needs is 'dancing shoes'. Back in the year 2000, the only way to get a decent pair was to buy them abroad.

One day, Sandip turned to Jameel and remarked, "You are in the leather line...can you make a shoe like this for me in Dharavi?"

Jameel jumped up and said "Yes! Why not?!"

He took a couple of sample shoes and tried to make copies.

"I worked very hard at it, but I could only make *kaam chalau* quality."

However, Sandip loved the vibrant colours and took the shoes anyway.

"That boosted my confidence and I kept trying to do better and better."

Slowly, people started asking for Jameel's shoes. And he was faced with a dilemma.

"I was getting the shoes made in Byculla, but was not happy with the result. I thought, if I am getting orders, I need to have my own workshop."

In 2005, Jameel quit his job and started his own business.

Dancing shoes are special shoes – they are very light, just like wearing socks. Each shoe must be custom-designed to the dancer's foot.

"We use leather, but nowadays, more of velvet and satin. Everything we need is available in Dharavi, except for satin."

With trial and error and perseverance, the quality of Jameel's shoes improved.

"People started saying, 'Why buy from abroad, I can buy just as good and cheaper from Jameel'. "

The young man opened a bank account.

One fine day, the bank called and offered a personal loan of ₹ 3 lakh. Jameel haggled for more. Ultimately, the bank disbursed ₹ 5 lakh.

"I took the money, borrowed some more from here and there and bought this room for ₹ 8 lakh."

This was in the year 2007.

Jameel's name and fame was growing in dance circles. One morning, he got a call from Priyanka Chopra's secretary.

"Madam wants to order your shoes," was the message.

Samples were sent over and a drawing of madam's foot requested. Three pairs of dancing shoes, ready to go!

And that was just the beginning. 'Shah Shoes' clients include Katrina Kaif, Kylie Minogue, Farah Khan, Kajol, and Hrithik Roshan.

"All the TV shows, like 'Jhalak Dikhla Ja' and 'Dance India Dance', order shoes from me," says Jameel.

And he insists on 'advance' because showbiz is a slippery business.

"I first take the money and then hand over the shoe," he grins. "*Baad mein paise ka lafda nahin.*"

Today, Jameel employs four kaarigars, and makes around sixty pairs a month. The shoes sell for ₹ 1,500 to ₹ 2,000, depending on the style.

And Jameel is a stylish young man now, himself.

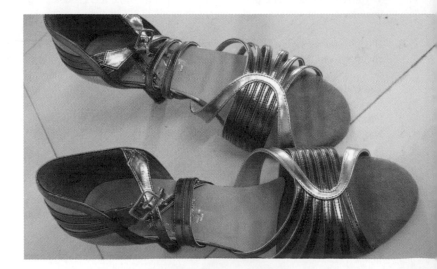

"I never knew English or how to use computers," he says. "Now I have a page of my own on Facebook."

Meanwhile, one of his brothers has joined the business while he supports two younger ones who are in school. His dream is to see one of them become a doctor and the other a lawyer.

"*Baaki unki marzi, unki kismet,*" he shrugs.

Jameel wants to expand his business further.

"I have just spent ₹ 2.5 lakh to renovate this place," he says.

The workshop is right above the living area. And there is a third floor, empty right now, but ready for use when orders increase.

Jameel's workshop is in 'Sector 5', the sector which the DRP has promised will be the first to be redeveloped. But that does not worry him.

"First of all, redevelopment *hone wala nahin hai.* But in case it happens, I have all the papers."

In any case, Jameel Shah has bigger dreams.

"There is a building in Juhu, with a view of the sea. I've always dreamt of buying a house there someday."

Well, who knows? The boy from Bihar who once slept in an auto now designs shoes for the stars. And Jameel believes if he can do it, so can any young boy who comes to the city today.

"*Mere jaise insaan ko agar life mein kuch karna hai to Dharavi mein aana chahiye.*"

You get a cheap place to stay, you get a job. What you make of yourself thereon depends on the strength of your hands, the passion in your heart.

Dharavi is the 'incubator' which made it possible.
A shack under a tin roof, a factory of dreams.

POOR
LITTLE
RICH
SLUM

CHAPTER 7

JAI HO

POOR
LITTLE
RICH
SLUM

"I prayed to God...give me so much work that I stay awake twenty-four hours."

Dressed in a spotless white kurta-pajama, and a flowing white beard, Mustaqeem Bhai looks more like a benevolent *maulvi* or social worker than a hardcore businessman. Yet, that's what he is.

Perhaps the most successful businessman, in all of Dharavi.

"*Sab mehnat aur imaandaari ka phal hai,*" he says modestly.

The story of his life reads like a fairy tale. Except, it did not happen 'once upon a time', but right here in Dharavi.

"I was born in 1957, in a small village of UP, in Rae Bareli district. My family owned a lot of land, but after zamindari was abolished, we fell on hard times."

Mustaqeem's father went to Kanpur and took up a job. He sent ₹ 10 home every month.

"I remember we used to go to the *haat* and buy 12.5 seer of wheat."

Ten-year-old Mustaqeem would carry the warm, freshly ground flour in a cloth bag on his head. For all of seven kilometres.

Somehow, the family got by.

Mustaqeem studied in the village school till Class 5. From Class 6 onwards, he went to a school in the next village, three kilometres away.

"There were some children who would buy sweets after school. *Hum sochte the, kash hamare pas chaar aane hote to hum bhi khate.*"

Nevertheless, Mustaqeem's focus was on his studies. So, he was surprised and dismayed to get a 'second division' in his final exam.

The twelve-year-old boy went up to the principal and declared, "*Mere saath zyadti hui hai.* I deserve a first class."

Mustaqeem requested the principal to allow him to sit for re-examination and let him prove himself.

"The re-exam did not happen, but principal sir gave me *shabashi.*"

But, by the time Mustaqeem reached Class 7, the family finances had worsened. There was no money for fees or books.

"I cried throughout summer and then declared to my mother: 'If I cannot study, I will go to Bombay and work there'. "

Luckily, Mustaqeem had a *jeeja* already working in Mumbai.

"My mother packed chapattis and *achaar* and we caught the Janta Express."

As he made his way to the station, villagers remarked, *"Itni chhoti umar mein kamane ja raha hai?"*

"I was scared but I had made a decision, so I put on a brave face."

"Bombay mein mamla hi alag tha."

Fresh off the train, Mustaqeem found himself sleeping on the footpath, in a lane behind Ahmed Mills in Kamathipura (Bombay's red-light district).

The year was 1970.

Quickly, Mustaqeem figured out the best thing to do – learn *silai ka kaam.* There were many people from his village in this line of work. One of them had made it 'big' – he now owned a small factory with 6-8 sewing machines. He took the young lad in as a helper, but without salary.

"I used to open the door of the factory, clean the machines and give *chai-nashta* to the tailors."

At the same time, Mustaqeem was keenly observing, and learning from them.

"I worked all day, long hours but *kaam se mujhe badi khushi milti thi.*"

At night, it was back to sleeping on the pavement. Some days, it would rain, and everyone would get up and run for shelter.

"There were days when we just stood all night, under the porch of one of the buildings."

But, nothing could deter Mustaqeem's enthusiasm for life. His positive attitude and helpful nature impressed everyone around him. After four months, the *maalik* of the factory gave him ₹ 25 on the day of Eid.

"I was so happy that day, I could not sleep all night," he recalls.

Mustaqeem quickly acquired a reputation for being a *tez* worker. He was eager to work with the best kaarigars to learn more and perfect his craft.

"When I was sixteen, I wrote to my father: 'Now you need not stay in Kanpur. I can support the family'. "

Mustaqeem himself began moving up in life. From Kamathipura, he shifted to Dadar, and then to Dharavi.

"On 1 April 1974, I took a 10 x 10 room on rent for ₹ 25 a month. I set up two sewing machines there and employed one boy to work under me."

It was all contract work – and initially not easy to get. For close to two years, Mustaqeem struggled to make ends meet.

"The worst part was that I even stopped sending money home."

But gradually, orders started coming in. Mustaqeem bought four additional machines and employed more tailors.

"*Main dua mangta tha ki itna kaam ho ki main chaubees ghante so-oon hi nahin*," he beams.

Mustaqeem got orders from exporters. They supplied the cloth, the sample and specifications. The tailoring unit had to deliver on a deadline and with precision.

This, Mustaqeem Bhai and his masters learnt to do very well.

"Par phir maine ek din socha, main sab kuch jaanta hoon – why don't I start exporting on my own?"

By this time, Mustaqeem had close to a 150 tailors working for him, and had even bought out the entire Banerjee compound where he was once a tenant.

"This compound has been very lucky and very good for me," he adds.

And that was proved once again, as Mustaqeem Bhai's export business took off.

In 1997, he procured his first order from America. How exactly it happened, he cannot explain.

"Jo cheez main sochta hoon, chahta hoon, Allah usey poora karta hai," he says with an enigmatic smile.

And that's how it continued over the next eleven years, with C M Craft going from strength to strength. At its peak, Mustaqeem Bhai's Dharavi factory was churning out 7-8 lakh pieces per year.

Then, there was a recession and the going got tough. There were buyer issues, quality issues, payment issues. But, somehow, C M Craft weathered the storm.

"Fashion keeps changing," he remarks, holding up an impeccably tailored ladies' top.

"Now, we focus more on quality and design."

As well as non-US markets like Mexico, Panama and Brazil.

As of 2011, C M Craft has achieved an annual turnover of ₹ 12 crore and employs four hundred people, all from in and around Dharavi.

Mustaqeem Bhai continues to live in Dharavi, although in a well-constructed high-rise building. His older sons will soon join the business, like his two brothers from the village.

Apart from business – which he is still involved in, hands on, Mustaqeem Bhai spends his time in community social work.

His message to the youth of today is simple: *buri cheezon se bachiye*. Cigarettes, alcohol, *beedi*, *paan* – all these are to be strictly avoided.

And above all, lead an honest life, caring for others as much as yourself.

"Kisi ko nuksan pahunchakar ya dhokha dekar maine kabhi koi kaam nahi kiya hai."

Because there must be *tehzeeb*, not just in art and poetry. But, life itself.

> "Moneylenders do big business in Dharavi. They give loans at two per cent weekly interest. One police officer – Sanjay Pandey – had cracked down on this practice some years ago but once he was transferred, everyone was back in business again.

— Anand Kumar*
Jewellery shop owner, Sakinabai Chawl

* Name changed on request

> "I came to Dharavi because that
> was the best I could afford."

The Ayyappan Idli Stall opposite Shankara Mattam temple in Matunga is an institution. On a Sunday morning, the crowd is swelling. Dosas are crisp, service is brisk.

If you stand at the stall for half an hour and calculate how much money it makes, you might just say to yourself, *"Naukri chhodo, yeh idli-dosay ka business achha hai."*

But, like all success stories, this one goes back a long way. Forty years, to be precise.

For Panju Swamy – owner of Ayyappan Idli Stall – has been in the 'hotel line' since the age of nine.

"I studied only till Class 3. Then I went to Madurai and worked at New Merit Hotel on Dindigul Road."

Eventually, the young man from Tirunelveli district landed in Mumbai. And did what most young men from South India did back then – get a job in an Udipi restaurant.

"I worked at Ramakrishna Hotel in Matunga as a *badli*. My brother used to work there earlier."

In those days, there was no 'salary'. You got food, you got shelter. When you wanted to go back to the village, the owner would give you ₹ 5.

In time, you became a 'dosa master' and got paid a princely ₹ 50 per month. Panju thus managed to save a small sum and invested ₹ 60 in a handcart.

"I used to stand in front of Mahavir Building in Matunga and sell *fanas* and *nariyal*."

In a couple of years, he had saved up enough to move to a shop – ₹ 1,000 deposit, ₹ 300 monthly rent.

But a few months later, the owner asked Panju to vacate, forcing him to once again sell his wares from the road.

In 1979, Panju got married and needed a place he could call 'home'.

"I came to Dharavi because that was the best I could afford."

In 1981, Panju took up a shop on rent once again. This time, he started selling *nashta*.

"*Aata* and chutney I brought from home on a cycle, rest I cooked in the shop."

Activity would start at 5 am, when his 'Mrs' would start grinding the fermented dal and rice mixture. By 6:30 am, Panju would be off on a cycle, to open shop.

"We were open from 7 to 11, then from 4 to 8 in the evening."

Business was good. In 1987, Panju moved to his present location. The 'ownership' (on *pagdi* basis) cost him ₹ 60,000. And ₹ 100 in monthly rent.

In 1995, Panju Swamy's teenage son joined the business. He added many new varieties to the menu – cheese dosa, spring dosa, Mysore dosa.

"We take catering orders also," says Panju.

The man has done well for himself. As the idli batter rises every morning, so have the fortunes of the Ayyappan Idli Stall.

And yet, Panju and his wife and his two sons (plus their wives and kids) continue to live in Dharavi.

"We have a big house, we have no problem," he says.

Three hundred and seventy-five sq ft in a redeveloped building is a penthouse by Dharavi standards. But compared to the rest of Mumbai…

"Actually I have not seen much of Mumbai," says Panju.

His entire world is sandwiched between Matunga and Dharavi. And he is a content man.

"Jo mere bhagya mein likha hai wohi to mujhe ayega."

Fate has brought hundreds of Panjus and Swamys to Dharavi. Few have risen to the same heights. But the humble idli batter rises and sustains them all.

More than 20,000 idlis are made every day in these 10 x 10 huts. To be sold by lungi-clad men carrying trademark steel canisters, covering every part of Mumbai city. And even as far as Pune.

An idliwalla can earn a profit of ₹ 200 to ₹ 250 per day for approximately four hours of work. That's enough to 'live well' in Dharavi.

To go beyond that, you need desire. A hunger to grow.

"Anyone can achieve what I have," says Panju. "But you have to work hard. I still stand at my stall twelve hours of the day…everyday."

And *that* is something few young men are prepared to do now.

The supply of young and hungry South Indian boys wanting to work in hotels is down to a trickle. It is labour from UP and Bihar who come seeking employment. Even they shy away from standing all day, in front of a hot *tawa*.

"I am in this line since childhood. I am not ashamed, even to wash plates," says Panju.

But for his grandchildren, he wants a 'better future'.

"Now I understand the value of education. I want my grandsons to study well and do something different."

"Dekhte hain, unke bhagya mein kya likha hai…"

While MBAs dream of entrepreneurship, entrepreneurs dream of white-collar jobs. The idli always appears fluffier, on the other side…

"

After the Babri Masjid riots in 1992, everything changed…Muslims started living in 'Muslim' areas, Hindus in 'Hindu' areas…. And situation was such that a small spark could start a fire.

But the mohalla movement started by Waqarbhai, Bhau Korde was the turning point.

We are proud that Dharavi has not seen riots again.

"

– Manik Prabhavati
Coordinator, Daya Sadan Community Centre, Dharavi

CHAPTER 9

HIDE
AND
SEEK

"If I die, no problem, my goodwill should live on..."

Sitting at his desk with export awards adorning the walls, a Voltas air conditioner humming in the background, Mushtaq Syed could be just another businessman. The difference is where he chooses to run his business.

In the heart of Dharavi, where his workers are.

Outside lies the heat and dust of humanity. To reach this office, you must navigate narrow lanes filled with people and animals, carts laden with fruits and freshly butchered meat.

Open gutters, shit and flies.

"I was born in Dharavi, but due to God's grace and the hard work of my father, Syed Ahmed Ali, I had a better life," says Mushtaq.

He and his three brothers, who jointly run INMA Enterprises, all grew up in Pali Hill – a posh residential area in Bandra.

"I may have friends who are film stars and designers, but every day I come here to the factory and I am reminded, not to take what I have, for granted."

The story of INMA starts three generations ago, when Mushtaq's grandfather migrated to Mumbai from a small village near Allahabad.

"Dharavi was just a marshland with some huts."

Mushtaq's grandfather was a broker of animal skins.

"He would get raw skin from the butcher and give it to traders."

There was plenty of space in Dharavi to store the skins. It was a 'dirty' business, full of sights and smells unwanted in 'civilised' locations.

In 1947, at the age of ten, Mushtaq's father, Syed Ahmed Ali, came to Bombay.

"They all lived in a tiny hut, 15-16 males together, no families."

Despite the miserable conditions, Syed Ahmed Ali had a passion for studies. Even as he helped his father in the trading business, he completed Class 10 in a night school. And also became an LIC agent, to earn something on the side.

Because Syed Ahmed Ali knew one thing: to dream big.

"This business is too small," he told his father.

"*Mashallah*, my father spoke very well and had a lofty vision," says Mushtaq. This scared his father no end.

"When I take the bus, why do you want to go by taxi," he would scold his son. "You earn ₹ 1 and want to spend 75 paise!"

"I want to earn ₹ 10 and spend ₹ 5," Ahmed Ali would shoot back.

And that is exactly what he did.

Ahmed Ali applied his mind and grew a business born out of survival instinct. Into an empire.

He realised that the market requirement was for skin from all over India. Far-flung locations from Kanpur to Kalyan, Nasik to Dhulia.

"My father borrowed some money and travelled to these places. He opened small branches in each city which would collect skins from the local butchers and send them to Dharavi."

Soon, Ahmed Ali became the biggest supplier of raw skin in Maharashtra.

The centre of action in the leather business is Chennai. That's where skins from all over the country are sent for curing and tanning.

Ahmed Ali borrowed ₹ 500 – a princely sum in those days – and boarded an Indian Airlines flight to Chennai.

"This created a very good impression, people there thought, 'He is a big man, we can trust him and deal with him'. "

But beyond spit and polish, Ahmed Ali's biggest asset was his heart.

"My father is a legend in Dharavi and in the leather industry," beams Mushtaq. "He was very good to people, very kind."

Ahmed Ali always paid his suppliers, even when the market was down.

His *usool* was, "If I die, no problem, my goodwill should live on."

It was this goodwill which brought Ahmed Ali enough business, enough liquidity to buy a house in Pali Hill.

"That move changed our life. We went to convent schools, studied in college. And, of course, we too became positive thinkers like him, and knew we had to do something in life."

By 1990, when Mushtaq and his brothers were ready to think of their own future, they realised one thing: the business would once again have to be transformed.

"Raw skin is a one-day-a-week business where you mostly work with butchers," says Mushtaq.

Not enough to keep four young men busy. Young, educated men who wanted to see the world, do bigger and better things in life.

"Education had opened our minds like a parachute...we knew life is not just about making money. You have to find something that interests you also!"

In 1990, Mushtaq and his older brother decided to get into the leather-garment business. A business they knew nothing about.

"We started with one tailor and one master," he recalls. "We also took stitching classes to understand the whole process."

Slowly, they mastered the art and science of quality. The right colour, finish, and every small detail, which turns an ordinary bag into an Item of High Fashion. Sporting a century-old brand name and supporting price tag.

In 1992-93, the brothers attended a trade fair in Germany, where INMA bagged its first export order. A small quantity from a designer seeking high-quality handcrafted leather goods.

"We never do bulk production, just 400-500 exclusive pieces," says Mushtaq with pride.

A family business, with that *personal* touch.

Irshad + Naushad + Mushtaq + Anwar = INMA. Four brothers dividing up tasks as per their talents and temperament.

"My elder brother is very good in marketing, you can listen to him 7-8 hours non-stop," grins Mushtaq. "I am good at purchase – that is where you can really make money if you are smart!"

A third brother studied footwear technology in England and has set up a shoe factory in Pondicherry. The youngest one is settled in the US and travels extensively, besides managing INMA's retail outlet in America.

Call it a 'slumdog millionaire' story, but one where an enterprise was built over blood, toil, sweat and skin.

Only to be torn down and *rebuilt* by the next generation, *reinvented* in the same location.

"This office where we are sitting today, it used to be a godown for salt."

Today there are no more skins to preserve, that era is over. The skins and tannery business has shifted from Dharavi, only cutting and stitching work continues.

And INMA too has bigger ambitions – of starting a design studio in Europe, of launching its own brand of shoes.

"I will have to shift the business at some point," admits Mushtaq.

But where will he get a place where the rent is so cheap, food is so cheap, and people can live right next to where they work?

He toys with the idea of shifting to Navi Mumbai. A modern factory set-up, with housing for the staff in the same premises.

"Yahan se jaane ko koi taiyyar hi nahin hai!" he sighs.

And maybe, that's not such a bad thing…

> " *Mumbai generates approximately 10,000 tons of waste every day, nearly 60-80% of the dry waste from the city (mainly plastic, cardboard, paper and metal) lands up in Dharavi for recycling in some form or the other.* "
>
> – Vinod Shetty
> Director, ACORN Foundation

CHAPTER 10

WELCOME
TO OUR
JUNGLE

POOR
LITTLE
RICH
SLUM

"There is something to learn from us."

Down a typical Dharavi lane, past chickens and chai shops, lies a tiny new enterprise. No plastic is recycled here, no leather is cut.

This is 'Be the Local', a travel and tour agency, which, true to its name, is run by two young locals – Fahim Vora and Tauseef Siddiqui.

Fahim is the talkative one, while Tauseef is quiet. They complement and supplement each other and, like many great business partners, they are also childhood friends.

"We are among the lucky ones in Dharavi who went to an English-medium school," says Fahim. "But, I was never interested in studies. I wanted to 'see the world'. "

At the age of sixteen, Fahim walked into a Domino's and took up a job as a pizza delivery boy.

"I told my parents, I have joined extra classes, and went to work every evening."

When he was found out, his father gave him a beating.

"Why can't you focus on studies," he said. "You have the chance I never had to make something of yourself!"

However, the bug of 'doing something' remained, so after completing Class 12, Fahim joined a call centre.

"I told my parents this would help me improve my English, so they let me work this time."

Side by side, he also enrolled for a BCom. It was in the second year of college, travelling between Mahim and Mumbai Central, that he saw an advertisement in the local train: 'Guide needed for foreign tourists.'

"This sounded different, more interesting than a call centre!"

So Fahim called the number listed and asked, "Where is your office?"

"Dharavi," came the reply.

Fahim was shocked. He had never heard of a tour company with an office in Dharavi. But hearing this gave him new confidence.

"I remember, I went for the interview on a Friday – wearing the traditional kurta-pajama dress we wear for prayers," he grins.

The owner of the tour company was a British man, who hired him on the spot. After a couple of days of training, Fahim was sent out to give foreign tourists a taste of the 'real' Mumbai. A tour of the city's most famous slum – Dharavi.

Fahim worked with the company for three months, but then he had a spectacular fallout with his employer. That's when he decided to start his own tour operation and approached Tauseef – a childhood friend – to join as partner.

Tauseef said, "This is a great idea – let's do it!"

And thus, 'Be the Local' tours was born in March 2010. The USP being that the tour would be given by a local – a student of Dharavi.

"First thing we did was create a website and some pamphlets. The investment was hardly anything; we used my savings from the previous job."

An empty godown behind his uncle's grocery store was converted into an office. Clients started coming in on word-of-mouth publicity. March 2010 was a great month with around thirty-five tour bookings.

Then the tourist season ended, along came the hot summer months. Business was negligible.

"We thought of closing down, because, after all, we could easily get a job and earn something at least!"

It was during this low phase that Fahim and Tauseef met Govindbhai, who operated around Gateway of India.

"He had his own clientele and used to give city tours to foreigners. Some of them, he would send for a tour of Dharavi as well."

But, just as business was taking off, Govindbhai fell severely ill and passed away. It was a big blow to the young duo.

"We had taken a small office in Colaba, but could not manage it anymore. We shut that and decided to focus on getting customers only through online marketing."

In the first year of operations, 'Be the Local' earned a modest ₹ 1 to ₹ 1.5 lakh and nominal profit. But, its 'success' cannot be measured only in terms of money.

"What we want to do is also dispel the negative image people have of Dharavi. We want them to see that people here are not beggars, they are hard-working and self-sufficient. There is something to learn from us!"

'Be the Local' also provides employment to college students from Dharavi. The student-guides get ₹ 500 for giving a two-hour tour, as well as a sense of pride and confidence.

"You see, ninety-five per cent of the people who come for a Dharavi tour are foreigners, so you get to practise your English with them," grins Fahim.

The tourist could be a backpacker or a CEO.

"After answering questions from such a variety of people, you are fully prepared for any kind of interview!"

Now that Fahim has completed his graduation, he has bigger dreams and plans.

"I know we are good, but we have not done enough marketing. We need to reach out to more customers!"

There is so much hope in these young faces.
So many dreams for the future.

Twenty years ago, Faheem and Tauseef might have started a small leather business, borrowing designs from foreign-made bags.

Today, they have started a service business, borrowing the idea from a foreigner.

The challenge is to not just replicate, but to stand for something different, and better. To not be known as the knock-off, but the 'real thing'.

And that's a challenge these young locals have accepted.

CHAPTER 11

QUEEN BEE

"I want my girls to go out,
work, see the world..."

It's 11 am and 'Rebe Rubi' tailoring centre is lifting its steel shutter. But, for owner Rani Nadar, the day began much earlier – at 5 am.

"My daughter Rubita leaves for school at 6:30 am, and Rebecca goes to college at 7. *Bachche log ka tiffin pehle banta hai.*"

Today, Rani has cooked *pongal* – with rice, moong dal, ghee, plenty of ginger and curry leaves.

"Price of everything going up and up, no?!" she sighs.

The next couple of hours go in completing household chores – washing *bartans*, *jhadu-pocha*, and more cooking.

"I buy whatever I need fresh, every morning. We don't have a refrigerator, no."

The house Rani lives in is typical Dharavi. One 10 x 10 ft room with a giant bed. In one corner stands a desktop computer and printer.

"We bought it for the girls," says Rani proudly. "There is Internet connection also, ₹ 400 a month."

Rani's brain is always calculating – how to get more work, how to get more cash. Even as she stirs dal in her tiny first-floor kitchen, her mind is on the activity in the workshop next door.

"My kaarigars come in from 9 am, I have to keep them busy!" she exclaims.

The monthly salary of a tailor who can stitch ladies' blouses is ₹ 18,000 per month. He needs to complete at least 12-15 pieces a day, to yield some profit.

"*Kaam ka tension rehta hai*," says Rani. But she smiles a lot, and keeps chugging along on cups of tea. The cup we're drinking is made by her husband.

"Yohan is a very helping nature person," says Rani. "Whatever I cook for lunch, he will also have for dinner."

With her business, her double-storey home and supportive husband, Rani is much better off than her neighbours in Bharati Chawl. But, she dreams of more.

"See, we have ground-plus-one right now. We can easily make it ground-plus-two, but to do that we need ₹ 6 lakh."

And where will that money come from? The informal system charges exorbitant interest rates, starting from two per cent per month.

"Even shops like Vijay Sales refuse to give EMI if you are from Dharavi," says Rani. "To buy computer, we paid ₹ 30,000 up front."

So it was quite a surprise for Rani when the State Bank of India sought her out, and *offered* a loan. This act of grace is a result of SBI opening an urban microfinance (MF) branch in Dharavi.

"Our focus is on the urban poor and particularly, woman empowerment," says Chief Manager Ashok Khaire. "Unless women progress, we cannot expect progress in society."

Like most microfinance lenders, SBI disburses loans to women self-help groups (SHGs). Where SHGs do not exist, the bank works with NGOs to set them up. And Rani – a well-liked, well-known member of the community – was an obvious choice.

"A *mahila mandal* has ten members and it's a *bachat* scheme," explains Rani. "State Bank gave us ₹ 50,000 loan, that's ₹ 5,000 per person."

The mandal meets twice a month, with members paying back ₹ 500 at a time. Some use the money to buy material for jobwork, others use it to fund household expenses or school fees.

"But everyone is very regular in paying back," says Rani, who keeps the accounts.

When the initial amount has been paid back, the women are eligible for a larger disbursement.

"This time we are expecting a loan of ₹ 2 lakh," says Rani proudly.

The money is certainly helpful to many of the members, but it is too little, too slow, for Rani. Rebecca needs a laptop, while Yohan wants to expand the workshop.

"Right now he gets jobwork for sherwanis and churidars, but we get them stitched elsewhere."

'Rebe Rubi' is always in demand – it's the only ladies' tailor in the neighbourhood. But Rani wants it to grow beyond that.

"In Ghatkopar, some boutique is charging ₹ 4,000 for stitching designer blouses. I'm sure I can do it better – and for less."

But how does she reach out, to such customers? And will her kaarigars really be able to deliver?

"The tailor who makes blouses went to his village for Eid and has not yet returned!" she exclaims. *"Abhi uska kaam bhi main dekh rahi hai."*

Over the years, Rani has tried training women in the neighbourhood.

"They do some hemming, but no one has learnt tailoring," says Rani.

Most of them are too occupied just leading their everyday lives. And, they are constantly busy with infants.

"Girls around here still marry young and have children with *tabar tod* speed," laughs Rani.

Something which definitely won't be the case with Rani's daughters.

"I want them to go out, work, see the world, gain confidence," says Rani. "But I'm not sure how and where…"

Meanwhile, Rani must worry about minor aches and pains – in her body, and in the business. The electricity bill is too high this month – over ₹ 5,000.

"They (municipality) don't check the meter properly.... *Jhopda area mein sab aisa hi chalta hai.*"

As a customer walks in and complains about a blouse which is falling off her shoulder, Rani has a light-hearted exchange with her.

"What can I do if you become fat and become thin every three months?"

She offers to fix it anyway, because that's what a ladies' tailor must do.

Dharavi cannot be fixed with a few quick stitches, but Rani continues to sew hopes and dreams.

Because that's what human beings must do, with the fabric of life.

POOR
LITTLE
RICH
SLUM

CHAPTER 12

WATER, WATER, EVERYWHERE

"It takes a lot of effort to
make a sale."

It is a truth universally acknowledged that an über-cool Internet
business must be located in Silicon Valley. In much the same way, if you
want to start a business at the 'bottom of the pyramid', the place to start
from is Dharavi.

Twenty-three-year-old Soaib Grewal is a graduate of the Rhode Island
School of Design. He could be working in London, New York or Paris.
Instead he is parked in Mumbai, setting up the operations of 'Waterwalla',
a social enterprise which aims to introduce clean-water technologies to
urban slums.

And the very first retail outlet of Waterwalla is located – where else – but in Dharavi.

The journey from Rhode Island to the social swampland of Mumbai began in April 2010.

"When I was in my third year of college, I met Anshu Vaish and Neil Parikh," says Soaib. "They had this idea of doing something for people who live in slums."

As pre-med students at Brown University, Anshu and Neil had a natural inclination towards public health. But, they also had an interest in economics and entrepreneurship. Darin Kurti and Nehal Doshi – both from Brown University – were also part of the founding team.

"We brainstormed a lot, on what kind of project to do," recalls Soaib. "Clean water kept coming up as a very important, very basic issue."

Reading reports about a problem is one thing, seeing the situation with your own eyes is quite another.

"Five of us who were working on this idea came down to Mumbai in July 2010," says Soaib. "We spent two months in Dharavi."

The water issue in urban slums is universal. Residents have illegal or semi-legal connections, because their homes are not officially recognised.

"Slums are always treated as transitional housing, but, in reality, these settlements extend for generations," observes Soaib.

That means young and old alike must survive on water unfit for human consumption. And yet, there is little or no awareness about boiling, filtering or purifying this water.

"We decided to take up the challenge of bringing clean-water technologies to slums," says Soaib.

But not in the classic non-profit mould. Because when you give something free, as charity, it has no value for the recipient.

"That is why Waterwalla is run as a social enterprise."

The team quickly realised that good, low-cost technology was available in India. The trouble was that it was not marketed to people in slums.

"Companies like Hindustan Unilever and Eureka Forbes have tried," says Soaib. But the slum market is very different from the middle-class."

Waterwalla explored many options, but the team realised that without local participation, selling would be an uphill task.

"Building trust and credibility in the community was crucial. We, therefore, decided to recruit a local entrepreneur as our franchisee," says Soaib.

And Dharavi was exciting because it already had vibrant markets and a culture of entrepreneurship. Inviting franchisees through the NGO network in Dharavi, Waterwalla zeroed in on the 'best candidate' – thirty-four-year-old Jitendra.

A wiry, neatly dressed young man, Jitendra was born and brought up in Dharavi.

"I used to work with Pratham (a well-known NGO in the field of education)," he smiles. "Then I became a distributor for ayurvedic medicines."

As a Waterwalla franchisee, Jitendra invests in inventory and marketing, while the company takes care of the rent and setting up the shop itself.

"Our role is to build the supply chain," says Soaib. "We have relationships with all the manufacturers."

The most important task is identifying the right technology. After studying thirty different devices, Waterwalla picked up the ones most appropriate for slum conditions. They are now on display in the tiny retail store.

"A lot of people come in and make enquiries," says Jitendra. "But it takes a lot of effort to make a sale."

It's really a question of mindset. The average Dharavi resident will happily spend ₹ 10,000 on a colour TV, but think a hundred times before buying a water filter.

"*Health is wealth, logon ke mind mein bithana padega,*" smiles Jitendra.

The sales staff plays an important role in making that happen. Jitendra has employed two women from the local community.

"I've found that they do a much better job than men," says Jitendra.

Waterwalla stocks a number of models – Bajaj, Eureka Forbes, and soon Tata will be added to the list. The top-selling model, surprisingly, is the most expensive one – costing ₹ 1,800.

"People see the purifier as an aspirational product, they save up and buy the best one we have to offer," says Soaib.

However, the most popular product sold by Waterwalla is Aquatab – a disinfectant tablet which costs as little as ₹ 1 per day.

"This is an entry point," says Soaib. "We know that once they get used to clean water they will invest in the purifiers."

You live and you learn, you adapt and you improvise. Because you are creating a new market. And Waterwalla knows Dharavi cannot be conquered in a day.

"We have plans to open more stores but for the next six months we will focus on this one, and fine-tune our business model," says Soaib.

Meanwhile, the $30,000 Waterwalla has raised from IBM, Dell, Brown University and personal sources, will keep operations going.

"Our model is based on the idea of sustainable change and that's what makes it so exciting," says Soaib.

That's the reason why Soaib has relocated to Mumbai, turning down conventional, more lucrative options.

"I always wanted to use my design knowledge for development," he says.

The blue logo jostling for the attention of Dharavi is a commitment. To take this idea to the bottom of every urban pyramid.

The journey has just begun.

tall
short
fat thin

SECTION 3

CAULDRON
OF CHANGE

*There are slums of desperation, and
there are slums of hope. Agents of hope
are everywhere in Dharavi, planting
seeds of change.*

CHAPTER 13

DIWAN-E-SLUM

POOR
LITTLE
RICH
SLUM

"... is the middle-class way of
life really better?"

There are no tables or chairs in the room. Visitors sit on the floor, just
like the man they have come to visit.

This is the *darbar* of Jockin Arputham, king among slum activists in the
city. A small man, wearing a blue half-sleeve bush-shirt. Above his bald
and shiny head, the Padma Shri citation hangs quietly on the wall.

Jockin was born on 15 August 1946.

"Wrong date," he chuckles.

Exactly one year later, India became independent, but Jockin and his family continued to lead a typical colonial life.

"My father worked for Kolar gold field in Karnataka," he recalls. "I had two servants to look after me – one carried my books and the other carried my water bottle."

But times changed and with it came a reversal of fortunes. By the time Jockin was in Class 7, the family was bankrupt. One day, Jockin came home from school and found there was no food to eat.

He ran away from home and became a 'street boy'.

Eventually, he landed up in Mumbai, at Janata Colony in Mankhurd (now known as Cheetah Camp).

"I had no roof over my head, no certainty where the next meal would come from."

Every day, he would look out for an empty veranda to sleep in at night. With the first azaan, Jockin would awake to bathe and wash his clothes. Lunch and dinner were whatever a kind lady might offer. Any remaining hunger pangs washed down by endless cups of strong tea.

Janata Colony was situated close to the upcoming Bhabha Atomic Research Centre (BARC). As major construction was going on, Jockin went there looking for work.

"I cleaned the toilets, removed the garbage," he says. "Soon I became a contractor with my own company called 'Lift 'n' Shift'. "

An enterprise born out of the simple need to survive, not any great plan or ideology.

Jockin worked hard and yet, he was free by 4 pm every day. To kill time, he started inviting the children of Janata Colony to sit with him – to sing and to play. Sometimes he would carry sweets in his pocket and distribute them.

In 8-10 days, three hundred kids were gathering around him every evening. In the process, Tamil-speaking Jockin learnt how to speak Hindi.

"The mothers were so happy, they kept feeding me tea and snacks," he recalls.

From a 'singing class' the activity soon morphed into an informal school where older children taught the younger ones. Under the watchful eye of Jockin 'sir'.

There was just one problem. The school was right next to a garbage dump and infested with mosquitoes. The municipal garbage collectors did not attend to it, despite reminders.

One fine morning, Jockin announced a 'picnic' for his kids. Each child was asked to bring along some newspaper.

"I made them each pick up 1 kg of garbage and said, 'Come, we are going to see the 'temple' of garbage'. "

The kids walked down 4.5 km, to Chembur. They dumped the garbage right outside the municipal office and headed back home.

When the office opened at 10 am, all hell broke loose. The police came searching for the mischief mongers.

"Arrest me," said Jockin. "But we will keep doing this every day, until you clean our garbage."

The municipal corporation got the message, and started doing its job.

This was the first of many community-roots campaigns by Jockin to improve the quality of life in slums. Children were the most important weapon in his arsenal.

"We cleaned toilets, cleaned drainage, improved roads," says Jockin.

In 1973, Jockin formed the Bombay Slum Dwellers' Federation. Meanwhile, he was also educating himself on slum history and its politics.

"The 'gift' of independence is a slum," observes Jockin.

Mankhurd Janata Colony was set up in 1947, to accommodate those evicted from slum areas in the city. The 'city' at that time ended at Sion.

Yet, in the early 1970s, the same Janata Colony once again faced an eviction notice. The land it occupied was now wanted by the BARC to build its staff quarters.

The battle Jockin fought against this eviction was a turning point in slum history. Janata Colony united under the banner of Bombay Slum Dwellers Federation and put up fierce resistance.

"At one time, there were 30,000 policemen trying to evict 70,000 residents," recalls Jockin. "On 17 May 1976, they came to arrest me – four times in one day."

Ultimately, the government gave up strong-arm tactics and offered a settlement. For the first time ever, slum dwellers were given alternate accommodation in a neighbouring location.

Every family received a 300 sq ft dwelling at a nominal rent of ₹ 1.50 per month.

This victory was proof that slum dwellers did not need 'outsiders' to fight for their cause. Jockin rechristened his organisation, the 'National Slum Dwellers Federation', the voice of the urban poor across India.

But this was the dark period of Emergency, when no voice was allowed to be heard. Jockin was in and out of jail, like many other activists.

"When you are in this line, you get connected to thinkers and activists in other countries. I was invited to give lectures and see their work."

So Jockin left India, and travelled the world. He visited Japan, Korea, Philippines, understood the condition of the urban poor in different cultures.

Jockin returned to India in 1978, after Emergency was lifted and all thirty-one cases against him were withdrawn. He continued to work against eviction of slum dwellers.

"I was a very militant leader back then," he recalls. "Short of killing, I did everything!"

If Jockin Arputham gave a 'call to action', 10,000 people would assemble within the hour.

"If we wanted, we could bring Bombay city to a halt on any day," he says.

Such was Jockin's popularity that he could disappear in a crowd when the police came looking for him. The ladies were so protective they would simply hide him inside the folds of their saris!

But, in 1985, Jockin underwent a change of heart. He gave up his militant stand and decided that the only way to work was through dialogue.

NSDF joined hands with an organisation called SPARC (Society for the Promotion of Area Resource Centres).

"For the first time, I found an NGO which believed in our cause and yet did not interfere in the way we worked," says Jockin. "Together we could be more effective."

The result of this peoples' movement was seen in small but tangible improvements. Slums started getting water, electricity connections and common toilets. A photo-pass was issued to identify residents of well-established slum colonies like Dharavi. As well as provide a more humane 'redevelopment'.

"As per law, even a criminal who has been given death sentence must be housed in an 8 x 8 ft space," he observes.

So how could a family of five possibly live, cook and sleep in a 150 sq ft area?

"Our strategy is to offer alternatives," says Jockin. "Can we do 'land sharing'? Can we do ground-plus-one structures? And so on."

And he has demonstrated how slum dwellers can be rehabilitated – without the state providing free homes – with experimental housing societies such as Markandeya. The only cooperative society in Dharavi built on land which has been leased from the BMC, in 1986.

'Friends' from Japan guaranteed the loan extended by the Bank of Baroda for construction by HUDCO. 121 families got 165 sq ft homes for a cost of ₹ 35,000 each, to be paid in instalments.

Although the houses are relatively small, there are some advantages. The passage, for example, is the lifeblood of any redeveloped building. The place where people meet and mingle with neighbours.

"We have given passages of 2 m, whereas most builders only give 1.1 m," says Jockin.

Nine other societies were formed, but only two of the projects were completed.

"There were many issues – including corruption," he shrugs.

Over the last five years, NSDF has helped shift 30,000 families squatting on railway land to new homes in Mankhurd and Govandi. But Dharavi is far more complex, nobody is willing to relocate.

"Dharavi is like a *janambhoomi* and *karambhoomi* for everyone who lives here," says Jockin.

The efforts continue. And more than putting up one or two or ten buildings, the focus has been on creating a *policy* change.

"The most important aspect is to involve the community and also consider the employment aspect," he says. "Only then will redevelopment be successful."

Which is why he is vehemently opposed to the Dharavi Redevelopment Plan.

"Moving slum dwellers to skyscrapers is doomed to fail."

As always, Jockin is ready with an alternative. A 'community-based' Dharavi redevelopment plan, starting in Sector 4.

"There is no question of getting 'permission' from anyone to do this. It is our right and we are exercising it," he declares.

The plan goes something like this: Sector 4 will be subdivided into forty sectors with 700 to 1000 families. Each sector would then create cooperative housing societies with a maximum of 150 families per society.

Jockin contends that not a 'single soul' would be shifted out.

Those residing in Dharavi prior to 1995, and in possession of valid documents, will get a free house. Others will pay the construction cost.

The free component will be funded by giving twenty-five per cent of the total space for commercial use.

"That is enough to generate the money required for redevelopment," says Jockin. "What DRP is proposing is driven by builders and their greed."

Jockin believes a self-development model would take 7-10 years, at the very least. But it's a short-enough time for those who've waited a lifetime. And yet, Jockin the crusader pauses for a moment, and reflects on his own life.

"People say slums are dirty, unlivable, inhuman…but is the middle-class way of life really better?"

As President of Slum Dwellers International – an organisation spread over thirty-seven countries – Jockin travels around the world. But it is the slum he still calls home.

A place where doors are always open.
People take care of each other, care for each other.
(It's true, not just a Bollywood cliché.)

As aspirations rise, so must the slum reach for the skies.
But let concrete not harden the hearts of its dwellers.

May Dharavi be ever-willing to welcome weary new country cousins.
Because it is their energy which powers its soul.

> I have been working on slum rehabilitation since 1972 and I can tell you, it is a very slow, very complicated process.
>
> SRA (Slum Rehabilitation Authority) schemes have not given desired results. The builders buy out committee members. The slum dwellers get a raw deal.
>
> – Adolf Tragler
> Founder, SRS (Slum Rehabilitation Society)

CHAPTER 14

THROUGH
THE
LOOKING
GLASS

POOR
LITTLE
RICH
SLUM

"People who live here know their rights..."

Nirmala Niketan College of Social Work is a neat, white building in a quiet street near Churchgate. Physically, it is far removed from Dharavi. But for the earnest-looking students and professors of the institution, Dharavi is a familiar place.

A place where generations of social workers have cut their teeth and earned their spurs.

Among the many who are familiar with Dharavi, there is Dr Jalindar Adsule. A man whose association with Dharavi began as a student and continued as an academic. What makes Jalindar unique is that he hasn't just worked from the outside.

He has lived in Dharavi and fought for Dharavi. He feels for it, from deep inside.

Unlike the vast majority who migrate in search of work, Jalindar came looking for a degree. The young boy born in a village in Satara district was inspired by the words of a TISS (Tata Institute of Social Sciences) professor at an NSS (National Service Scheme) camp.

Unfortunately, Kolhapur University declared the results late that year, so he could not join TISS.

"I did not want to go back to my village, but I needed some place to stay in Bombay," recalls Jalindar.

So, he took admission in the law course, purely for the hostel facility. But most of his time was spent in student politics. During one of the many *morchas* he took part in, Jalindar was arrested.

"When my brother in the village heard about it, he came to Bombay and said, 'Enough is enough. This is not the social work we sent you here to do!'"

Luckily, around the same time, there was an advertisement in the newspaper from Nirmala Niketan for its Master's in Social Work (MSW)

programme. The ad promised a degree and employment. Jalindar immediately applied and was accepted in June 1979.

The course comprised three days of lectures and three days of practicals. That is how Jalindar was first exposed to Dharavi, working at the municipal school. But that was not enough for him.

Jalindar knew some people from Dharavi, thanks to his student activist days. Through them, he started working with some local organisations.

"That was the beginning of what you can call my 'intervention' in Dharavi."

Jalindar helped form a youth group, and two of the members of that group later came to Nirmala Niketan for a para-vocational course in social work.

After completing his MSW, Jalindar joined Nirmala Niketan as part of the project staff. At that time, there was a project called the Bombay Slum Citizens' Development Project. Although the area of work was in Santa Cruz, Jalindar remained connected with Dharavi.

"I always felt that working in just one slum is not going to help, you need to have a network with others as most of the slum problems are common."

Thus Jalindar helped in forming the Akhil Mumbai Zopadpatti Sanghatna, with members from slums across north Bombay.

Meanwhile, he was getting a taste of the bitter medicine every new arrival in the city had to swallow. The difficulty of getting a house. Once again, Jalindar enrolled for a degree in law and got hostel accommodation. But at the end of three years, the problem remained.

"I decided that the best place to stay is Dharavi," he grins.

For a monthly rent of ₹ 500 (no deposit), Jalindar finally had a residence of his own in the city. A place he could live in with his newly wedded wife.

From this vantage point inside the slum, he closely observed the many social experiments being conducted.

There were organisations like Shramik Vidyapeeth started by Bilkees Latif, wife of the former Governor of Maharashtra. This government-supported NGO had a number of technical and vocational programmes for members of the community.

"They identified youth from 15 to 45 years from all over Dharavi and arranged sessions on Sundays. I gave them extensive training in various areas, including housing legislation, functions of BMC (Bombay Municipal Corporation), police station, etc."

Some of the students of this programme later formed the Dharavi Vikas Samiti. Others joined existing NGOs and local mandals. A couple were even elected as corporators.

The cadre of socially aware citizens of Dharavi was slowly growing. The residents were realising the meaning of 'people power'.

Another organisation working tirelessly in Dharavi was PROUD (The People's Responsible Organisation of United Dharavi), a well-funded NGO with different wings working on different issues. A faculty member at Nirmala Niketan – Prof Dominic D'Souza – invited Jalindar to join his team.

The goal was to evaluate the impact of work done by PROUD, between 1982 and 1987.

"We went from area to area, speaking to people. Understanding what are the issues, how these issues are discussed, how decisions are taken, what happens after that!"

The study gave Jalindar a deeper understanding of Dharavi and its complexities.

In 1985, SPARC (Society for the Promotion of Area Resource Centres) emerged as a force in Dharavi. The vice-principal requested Jalindar to place some of Nirmala Niketan's students with the organisation.

"We were excited to associate with SPARC because in the beginning they were influenced by the work of Paulo Freire – the renowned Brazilian educator. We were teaching this material in class, but our students were not getting practical exposure."

SPARC gave the young students of Nirmala Niketan more than they might have bargained for – the job of conducting a complete survey of Dharavi. With the help of local volunteers, and Jalindar's guidance, the survey was conducted successfully.

This was just around the time that Prime Minister Rajiv Gandhi had visited Dharavi and sanctioned a grant of ₹ 35 crore for its upgradation.

"There was a lot of hope among people; they wanted help in forming housing societies and take advantage of redevelopment under PMGP (Prime Minister's Grant Project)."

But like all well-intentioned schemes, this one too failed to turn the ugly duckling into a swan. A few buildings did come up, like pimples on a pockmarked cheek. For the majority, life remained unchanged.

In 1991, Madhav Chavan and Farida Lambay (former vice-principal of Nirmala Niketan College) started a literacy mission called Pratham. Jalindar worked as a volunteer and trainer with the programme, with responsibility for G South Ward (Dharavi).

In 1993, when Bombay was rocked by communal riots, Dharavi faced a tough test. Luckily, sanity prevailed as the many social workers, NGOs and citizens formed mohalla committees to 'keep the peace'.

"I conducted a number of sessions for these mohalla committees, on how we can all live and work together," recalls Jalindar.

At this time, Nirmala Niketan College also started a project called Salokha – Centre for Communal Harmony, where Jalindar was involved.

In 1993-94, Jalindar decided to do his PhD. The topic he chose was apt: 'Housing Problem in Bombay and Role of NGOs'.

"My guide asked me to do a complete case study on Dharavi. So I went into the depth of who came here first, how slums spread and the dynamics of each slum – who plays what kind of role, relationship with police station, etc."

Ultimately, the complete case-study idea was abandoned – it was too complicated. Instead, Jalindar did a case study of SPARC and Markandeya Cooperative Housing Society, a new model in slum redevelopment.

The addition of 'Dr' to his name did not lessen Jalindar's involvement with Dharavi as an activist and grassroots worker. He was a driving force behind CATCH – the Community Animators Training Programme for Communal Harmony. Not only that, but in 2005, when a series of demolitions were taking place all over Mumbai, he formed a network of NGOs working on housing problems – the Awaas Adhikar Sanyukt Kruti Samiti.

"We succeeded in getting the voice of the slum dwellers heard," he says.

And once again, he is doing the very same – amplifying the voice of the people opposing the Dharavi Redevelopment Project. As a member of the high-power steering committee recommended by the Bombay High Court to study the slum problem in Mumbai, he has raised various issues and concerns that residents have with DRP.

So, what do Dharavi residents actually want? Practical solutions, concrete action.

No pipe dreams.

"One thing I notice is that Dharavi has its own, very strong leadership. People who live here know their rights, they are socially and politically aware."

Local residents stand for and win municipal elections, unlike other slums where candidates are usually outsiders.

"The work done by so many NGOs in Dharavi over the last thirty years is reaping results now," adds Jalindar.

There is no dearth of community centres, vocational centres, service centres and other locally led organisations in Dharavi. Besides, the typical Dharavi resident is no longer the desperate economic migrant.

"There are many people like me who are well-educated and work as lecturers, police officers, social workers, in banks and for the government."

While Jalindar himself took a house on rent in Ulhasnagar and shifted out of Dharavi in 1986, others have not been so lucky. Or as determined. If all they can afford is two hours outside the city, they would rather stay put here.

In a scientific laboratory, you conduct experiments and instantly get some kind of result. Readings and measurements, success or failure.

In the field of social science, things are never as clear. Dharavi has long served as a laboratory for practitioners of development and change. Experiments are ongoing, though measurements are elusive and 'results' unclear.

Still, Dharavi continues to fascinate social scientist from India, and every part of the world. A wonder of the urban jungle, the Taj Mahal of slums.

CHAPTER 15

MAY
THE FORCE
BE WITH
YOU

POOR
LITTLE
RICH
SLUM

> "There is a lot of anger and
> sadness within..."

The train is near, very near.

So near that when it rumbles past, you can *feel* it in your bones.

Lying on a makeshift bed is an elderly man. He is silent and still as a dozen needles are carefully stuck into his lower back.

The doctor finally looks up from his labours and smiles. Another patient awaits on the opposite bed. And several others, in the tiny waiting area outside.

It's just another Monday evening at the Barefoot Acupuncturists Clinic located in the heart of a slum colony on the tracks near Bandra station. The locals call it 'Social Dawakhana' and gingerly make enquiries.

"*Maine suna hai dard ka idhar achha ilaaj hota hai*," says Naseema, a thirty-something mother of two.

Ninety per cent of the patients at Barefoot Clinic are suffering from some kind of chronic physical pain.

"Life in the slum is not easy," says Walter Fischer, chief acupuncturist and co-founder of the clinic.

Walter Fischer is a little crazy. He believes that sticking needles into people can change the world.

"I have done many things in my life – sold chemicals, then started a bar and restaurant business. But at the end of the day, all of it was meaningless."

At the age of thirty-five, Walter stumbled upon Chinese medicine and decided *this* was his calling in life. He spent the next five years training to be an acupuncturist – first in Switzerland, then in China.

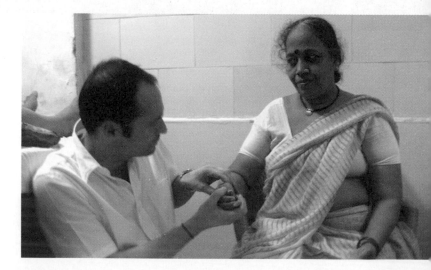

"But what I really always wanted to do was social work," he says.
Was it possible to use the skill of acupuncture for the greater common good?

"A friend of mine knew of a foundation in India working in the slums," says Walter. "I contacted them and offered to hold a free medical camp."

Thus, in May 2007, Walter Fischer and Jacques Beytrison came to Mumbai to work with CSSC (Centre for Study of Social Change). That's where they met Ujwala Patil, a young woman who was deputed as their translator and assistant.

Ujwala grew up in the slums of Bandra East but never really wanted to be a social worker.

"I always wanted to do my own business," she laughs.

Like many young girls, Ujwala completed her schooling and started working part-time at a beauty parlour. At the same time, she became a volunteer at CSSC.

"Actually my mother forced me," recalls Ujwala. "She said, 'Better than sleeping in the afternoon, learn something new'!"

At CSSC, Ujwala was trained to work as a pharmacist. The NGO ran twenty clinics in slums across the city with doctors who volunteered their time. When the coordinator of this activity quit CSSC, Ujwala quickly filled his shoes. It fell on her to coordinate Walter's visit to India as well.

"I had never heard of acupuncture before I met Walter," she admits. "Initially, our health workers went door to door, looking for patients!"

The first free camp conducted by Walter and Jacques went on for twenty-five days. It was a big success. Walter returned to India in August 2007, to set up a permanent clinic. Ujwala's mother – a social worker – helped them find a small place, free of charge.

"My brother paid the electricity charges, Walter bought the needles," says co-founder Ujwala.

And thus, in January 2008, began the work of 'humanitarian acupuncture'. Treatment for those who cannot afford it – people living in Mumbai's slums.

"It was a very small clinic," says Walter. "Just enough space for two beds and two of us to stand in between!"

Patients started trickling in – maybe 20-30 a week. Within a few months, word spread and there were fifteen people coming in every day. By this time the clinic had a name – 'Barefoot Acupuncturists' – and Walter hired an assistant.

Acupuncture is effective in ninety per cent of cases, but results take time. The process starts with an intimate personal and medical history of the patient, during the very first visit.

"We look for the root-cause of the problem," says Walter. In Chinese medicine, everything boils down to *qi* – or 'life energy'. If the flow of qi is blocked, it manifests as disease. The physical body affects the mental state, just as the mental body affects the physical state.

"Pain is the most common problem – back pain, foot pain, joint pain. But the real issue lies elsewhere," says Walter.

Lack of sleep is the biggest problem; there simply isn't enough space in the typical 10 x 10 hutment.

"Life is even harder for the women," adds Ujwala. "There is a lot of anger and sadness within that creates pain in the body."

It's little wonder then, that three days of the week at Barefoot Acupuncturists are reserved exclusively for female patients. And that is also the main reason that the clinic charges just ₹ 20 per visit.

"Women will spend any amount for the husband and children, but rarely on themselves," says Ujwala.

What's more, a patient requires a minimum of five sittings, to gauge whether the treatment is working. Evidently it is working, because, in May 2009, the clinic shifted to bigger premises in the Siddharth Nagar slum, to cater to more patients.

So, if the service is practically free, how does Barefoot manage to function? An aid agency and some individual donors are supporting the cause.

"I believe that as long as we do something truly and with our heart, we will always find money," says Walter.

The amount needed to run the clinic is a modest ₹ 1.2 lakh a month, which includes overheads and salaries for ten staff members. A second clinic opened in the slums along the railway tracks in Bandra (E). A third clinic recently opened near the T-junction in Dharavi.

The problem is that the same handful of acupuncturists and assistants juggle duties between the clinics. And that worries Walter.

"What if I am not there tomorrow?" he muses. "All this work would be for nothing!"

Walter's dream is to make the community self-reliant. Barefoot Acupuncturists is exploring the idea of working with an NGO which is active in thirty-seven villages. The idea being to train rural health workers, especially women, in the art and science of acupuncture.

"I also want to write a handbook on 'humanitarian acupuncture' to deal with the problems unique to slums and villages," adds Walter.

On the one hand, Walter is an idealist and a dreamer. But he is also a very practical man.

"We treat 50-70 people a day, when there are 300 million who need it. So why are we doing this, you might ask!" he exclaims.

Because he believes that positive thinking and positive action make a difference in the world. A world where slums are seen as feeble and diseased organs in the body of a city.

But, is that really true?

You don't need to be an acupuncturist to feel the 'life energy' – strong and vibrant – in Dharavi. The question is, will redevelopment improve the flow of urban 'qi'?

CHAPTER 16

WASTE
WARRIORS

> "We cannot change the harsh
> realities of life."

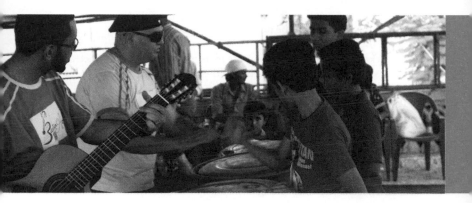

Aldo di Julho looks every bit the musician. It's not just the guitar he carries, but the way he carries himself.

"My Engleesh very very bad," he laughs.

But it does not matter, for they are gathered here – this jolly man from Brazil and a dozen boys from Dharavi – to speak a universal language. The language of music.

The 'studio' is an open-air terrace. The 'instruments' are plastic drums, pipes and masking tape.

The tape is skilfully wrapped around the tip of each pipe, to make drum-sticks.

Coca-Cola cans filled with sand create the percussion.

"Ready…1…2…start!"

A dozen young hands start beating their sticks on the drums. Sixteen-year-old Afsar is one among them.

On any other day, he would be spending his afternoon in the nearby Mahim creek, searching for plastic bags, plastic drums and scrap iron. He is one of the few hundred ragpickers who live and work in and around Dharavi.

Doing a job that needs to be done, but no one else wants.

"Ragpickers are not just poor, they are invisible," says lawyer and activist Vinod Shetty. "Nobody wants to talk to them, engage with them."

Ragpickers are survivors. Destitutes and dalits, abandoned women and juveniles on the run.

"Ragpicking is the one thing you can do in the city, to fill your stomach," says Vinod.

All you need is your own two hands.

Vinod practises in the Mumbai High Court, where fat-cat corporate cases are aplenty. But, his heart beats for the kind of people who don't know their rights and who cannot afford his fees.

From his tiny office on the third floor of a residential building in Bandra (E), Vinod coordinates the activities of ACORN (Association of Community Organisations for Reform Now), a registered charitable trust working in twelve countries across the world. In Mumbai, the focus of ACORN's work is the upliftment of ragpickers through 'Project Dharavi'.

"As a labour lawyer, my initial idea was to organise and unionise the ragpickers," says Vinod. "But I realised that would not work."

Unlike mill workers, ragpickers are lone wolves. They live around garbage dumps, and landfills, under pipes and bridges.

"Many of the ragpickers are mentally disturbed, or addicted to drugs," he adds.

The challenge was to first win the trust of the ragpickers and then create a community they could belong to, working for their needs.

"The very first thing we did was to start identifying ragpickers and give them identity cards," says Vinod.

Very soon, Vinod realised that the real victims of the ragpicking trade were children. Many simply tagged along with their parents as 'helpers', others had no family at all and worked for survival.

"Going to school was out of the question for these kids!" says Vinod.

ACORN set up a small office, right next to the creek where most of the ragpickers assemble and fish for plastic waste. After work, the kids were encouraged to drop by and have some fun.

"We organised informal music classes, sports and games," says Vinod.

This led to the idea of 'Dharavi Rocks', a joint project between ACORN Foundation and Mumbai's most happening club – blueFROG. Musicians from across the world perform at blueFROG every month. On their agenda now is a stop at Dharavi, to hold workshops and to perform with ACORN kids.

The result is clearly visible.

As Aldo di Julho waves his hands and taps his feet, the boys effortlessly follow the beat. Next month, they will perform at blueFROG, along with Taufiq Qureishi, to raise funds for ACORN.

And, more importantly, raise awareness about Dharavi and the role it plays in supporting the city.

"I call the ragpickers 'green-collar workers'. They are making a heroic contribution to our lives, yet we see them as a burden to society."

ACORN also works with elite schools, bringing children on field trips to Dharavi to understand what waste management and recycling is all about.

"When kids see the work of the ragpickers, they feel inspired to do their bit at home," says Vinod.

Meanwhile, fun, games and musical expression apart, ACORN is doing its bit to get young ragpickers into the system. After much persuasion and remedial classes, some of the kids have recently been admitted to school.

Afsar is one of them.

The sixteen-year-old is now enrolled in Class 3 at the local municipal school. He attends classes from 7:30 in the morning till noon. Yet, he continues to spend his afternoons at the Mahim creek, scouring for plastic waste.

The ₹ 150 he earns each day help support his four brothers, two sisters and mother. Since Afsar's father passed away two years ago, he is the main breadwinner of the family.

"We cannot change the harsh realities of life," admits Vinod. "But we want kids like Afsar to live and work in better conditions."

And that can only happen when NGOs and the state machinery work together.

"We want the government to impose a cess of one per cent on each bottle of Bisleri sold," says Vinod. "That money should go towards giving these ragpickers a regular income, gloves and training on how to handle toxic waste!"

Until that happens, ACORN will continue its individual effort. Bringing joy, confidence and hope into the lives of these young workers.

"We plan to release an album called the 'Dharavi Project' with tracks by our boys," beams Vinod. "All the musicians who have conducted workshops for them have also promised to contribute."

Aldo di Julha – the Brazilian 'baiao' – is one of them. But for now, he is busy with his pupils. They are banging down their sticks, with carefree abandon.

These drums of Asian Paints are, for this moment, magical objects producing magnificent sounds. In that moment, anything and everything seems possible.

"Aage main ek bada insaan banna chahta hoon," says Afsar. *"Bada aadmi ban kar jhopad patti walon ko building mein ghar dena chahta hoon."*

Because a life lived only for oneself is the biggest waste of all.

CHAPTER 17

STRENGTH
OF
CHARACTER

"It's all about discipline."

The faint smell of *dhoop* hangs in the air.
It clings to the barbells and the dumbbells and every other equipment.

"We do *arti* here every morning," says Praveen Sakpal.

For this is a temple where the faithful flock to worship the body.
Where Praveen is not just a trainer, but God of all things.

Gurudutt Gymnasium is the pride of Dharavi. Displayed at the entrance
are photographs of not one or two, but eight boys from this gymnasium
who have 'made it' as bodybuilders.

Their guru is Praveen.

"I grew up watching my father use dumbbells and I knew what is biceps and triceps," says Praveen.

At the age of seventeen, he too started exercising. But the turning point in his life came when he met his guru, Madhukar Thorat.

"*Unke under training chalu kiya to aisa laga bhagwan mil gaye,*" he says.

It happened by chance, on the day of Holi. Praveen's regular gym was shut, so he came to Sree Gym in Nehru Nagar (Kurla) for a workout. There, Madhukar 'sir' put him through a punishing routine.

"I told Madhukar sir, 'I want to become a bodybuilder, make me your student,' " recalls Praveen.

Sir replied, "Come tomorrow at 6 am and we will see."

Looking back, Praveen knows sir was testing him.

"He knew I would barely be able to walk and did not expect to see me," he grins.

But the next morning at 5:30 am, Praveen was at Madhukar sir's doorstep. The guru was so pleased he took in the *chela*. Treating him like his own son.

"I put my heart and soul in training," says Praveen. "I was at the gym from 5 am to midnight."

Hard work, hard training and commitment brought results. In 1991, Praveen won the sub-junior title in Mumbai. The same year, he went on to win the state-level gold medal.

"Later, I competed in senior (under twenty-one) category and won a gold medal in Bombay, in Maharashtra and national level also," he adds.

Bodybuilding had another positive outcome. Praveen joined the railways' clerical division under the 'sports quota' in 1995. That's where he met a committee member of the Gurudutt mandal, who offered him a second job.

"Come and train at our gym and train our youngsters also," the man offered.

Praveen badly needed the extra cash.

"*Us time maine apna alag se room le liya tha,*" he recalls. "The instalment was ₹ 5,000 per month."

Thus it was that Gurudutt Gym got a new 'sir'. A sir who would not just do his job but change lives. And bring much glory to Dharavi.

"When I joined Gurudutt Gym, it had a tin roof and some very basic equipment," recalls Praveen. "Boys came to workout but they had no guidance."

The first thing Praveen did was to create a system. He hired three additional trainers, brought in better equipment and raised the fee from ₹ 10 to ₹ 50.

"Our membership did not fall, in fact it shot up to 800!" he says.

'Praveen sir' became the man everyone wanted to train with, and emulate.

"I took a handful of boys who were serious about bodybuilding and worked day and night with them."

Lalit Koli and Kiran Koli were the first two 'stars' to emerge. They created hungama in Mumbai by winning the Junior Mr India title.

Hearing of this, a boy from Kolhapur – Suhas Khamkar – came to Mumbai. He took a room on rent in Dharavi and started training under Praveen sir.

"Suhas won a medal at the Asian level. *Uske jaise aur ladke mere paas aane lagey!*"

The first thing Praveen asks every boy who wants to be a bodybuilder is: "Are you serious?"

Bodybuilding is 'hard core'. You start training at 6 am and go on till midnight – hours and hours of freehand workouts, weight-training and posing practice. Not to mention 'road running', tanning, massages and most importantly, eating, eating and eating.

That's why any boy who says he is serious must then ask himself: "Can I afford it?"

The dietary requirements of a bodybuilder can cost ₹ 1,500 to ₹ 2,000 per day. That includes forty egg whites, chicken, fish, salad, juices, fruits and vitamins.

"I prescribe 3 kg of apple – that's ₹ 300 to ₹ 400 a day on apples alone," says Praveen.

Over and above all that, you need expensive imported protein supplements. The goal is to make the body all-muscle, no-fat. But there is a price to pay, both in terms of cash and commitment.

"Majority of the boys I advise should do fitness workouts, not bodybuilding. But a few stubborn ones still go for it."

Because they dream of medals and titles, like Praveen did.

The thirty-six-year-old bowed out of competitive bodybuilding in 2004, due to injury. But the results he has achieved as a coach are equally astounding.

As the old jungle saying goes: *"Gurudutt Gym ayega toh Mr India banega."*

And nor without reason. Yogesh Nikam, Amar Khandar, Sachin Patil, state champion, national champion – the success stories are many and memorable.

"Two of our Dharavi boys – Murugan and Sachin Patil – have won gold medals in the handicapped category!" adds Praveen.

What he is really proud of is the fact that eight of his boys have got jobs in the railways under 'sports quota'. An employer who demands just four hours of work a day and grants three months of leave before major competitions.

"Bodybuilding is a sport where you spend and spend but hardly earn anything," rues Praveen. "But if you get a medal at the national level you can get a government job."

And that makes all the hard work, worth something.

Even the boys who do only regular workouts are benefiting. Boys from Gurudutt Gym are in demand at fitness centres like Gold's Gym. The average salary of a trainer is ₹ 20,000 to ₹ 25,000 per month.

"Around twenty of my boys have got such jobs," reveals Praveen.

Direct outcomes are wonderful, but the influence of Praveen sir goes much beyond what can be quantified. Countless parents in Dharavi see him as their saviour.

"Ja, Praveen sir ke paas ja, kuch seekh," they tell their teenage sons.

Praveen sir's rule is simple: "If you want to join my gym, leave all your 'habits'. Cigarette, alcohol, gutka – strictly not allowed."

"It's all about discipline," he says. "Come on time, bring your towel, no *dadagiri* – no matter who you are."

Tough love is the secret of Praveen sir's popularity. The boys worship him and they want to be like him. This is the love which has kept Praveen in Dharavi, for fifteen years.

"I got an offer from Talwalkar's for a job at ₹ 40,000 per month," he says. "But, I cannot leave Gurudutt Gym. This is like my home."

That feeling is reciprocated by the Koli community, which owns the five-decade-old gym.

"Gurudutt mandal has supported me every step of the way," says Praveen.

The mandal took a loan to construct a more modern building, get better equipment and install air conditioners. The gym now charges a fee of ₹ 400 per month, but the boys just keep coming.

"In every gali of Dharavi you will see people with *zabardast* bodies," says Praveen. "It's all because of Gurudutt Gym."

Confidence is a cult of belief.
If you can build your body, you can build your life.

POOR
LITTLE
RICH
SLUM

CHAPTER 18

WOMAN
POWER

"Auraton ko kamzor na samjho..."

Hanifabi has lived in Dharavi since 1958, when she was three years old.

"That time there was a lot of water problem in Dharavi. My mother and grandmother used to get water from Wadala and Antop Hill and sell it here."

Hanifa and her three sisters were brought up by these ladies.

"My *abbu* died when I was young and my mother married again. But even my stepfather ran away after some time."

Hanifabi was married off at the age of fifteen – as per custom – to Syed Bashir, who hailed from 'Madras side'.

"The time was such that girls were not safe, even in their own homes, *yeh pura real jungle jaisa tha.*"

Hanifabi's life was no different from thousands of other women's in Dharavi. It was tough, with four daughters and a son, all growing up in a tiny hut. Syed's income as a taxi driver was never enough, so Hanifabi chipped in.

"I used to wash bartans, do *malish* for women after delivery and even started selling dress material."

But, that's the story of countless women in Dharavi; there was *something* more to Hanifabi. And that was a desire to reach out and help others.

Anytime a lady in the neighbourhood had a delivery, Hanifabi would rush her to hospital. If a case of wife-beating came to her notice, she would make it her business to sort things out.

But, it was a case of murder in her own building – a society built under the SRS (Slum Rehabilitation Scheme) in the year 2000 – which proved to be a turning point in Hanifabi's life.

"A man living on the floor above us killed his wife and then burnt her body. When we took the girl to hospital, the police said it is an accident, but then why did she not scream for help?"

Hanifabi's own daughter Salma, suffering in a bad marriage, was also very affected by the incident.

"*Jo Shaina ke saath hua hai wo mere saath ya meri bachchi ke saath bhi ho sakta hai,*" thought Salma.

But, what could two uneducated women do about it? The police chowki was a place everyone was afraid of.

"Even if a woman is bleeding and beaten black and blue, police say it is a 'family matter' and refuse to register an FIR. If you go with the complaint instead they warn – *lafde mein mat pado.*"

Allah is merciful, and it is at the darkest hour that He sends an Angel of Hope. That angel came in the form of Nayreen ma'am of SNEHA (Society for Nutrition, Education and Health Action).

"Nayreen madam told us, 'You must fight for your rights.' "

To do that, you have to first *know* your rights. And that's the knowledge SNEHA has imparted to Hanifabi, Salma and hundreds of other women in Dharavi.

"We formed Aashiyana Mahila Mandal after getting training from SNEHA in all the laws, especially Islamic law," says Salma. "We used to call all the women in the neighbourhood and explain to them also."

Adds Hanifabi, "*Dimaag to tha par gussa bhara hua tha, samajh nahin thi.*"

"At SNEHA we learnt the right methods, how to talk to people in authority and get work done."

Today, both Hanifabi and Salma are local firebrands. Battered women knock at their door at two in the morning, seeking help. And Hanifabi as well as Salma are ever ready, to fight the good fight.

That is the spirit in which SNEHA itself was conceived, in 1999. As Dean and Head of Neonatology at Lokmanya Tilak Municipal Hospital, Sion, Dr Armida Fernandez routinely had patients from Dharavi.

Many women came in with fractures, due to domestic violence.

"We treated the fracture," says Dr Fernandez, "but we had to send these women back to the same abusive husband."

What could be a more *long-term* solution? Thus was born SNEHA, with an agenda centred on violence against women and better nutrition for mother and child. And, creating catalysts for change.

At the SNEHA field office in Chhota Sion Hospital, 20-25 domestic violence cases come in every month. But it wasn't always like this. People used to think beating one's wife is a normal part of being a *mard*.

"Initially, we trained a hundred women from the community on what is violence and why it is not to be suffered in silence," says Dr Wasundhara Joshi, executive director of SNEHA.

The idea is not to 'punish' husbands and put them behind bars. The *threat* of police action is usually enough to scare him to come and resolve the *jhagda* through counselling.

"We give both sides a chance to tell their side of the story," says Jenny, a young counsellor at the centre. "At the joint meeting we negotiate and reach a 'settlement' which both parties sign."

The women mostly want men to stop drinking, stop beating, and to give them enough money to run the household. The men want wives not to shirk from their cooking duties and to limit visits to the *maika*.

Sounds simple enough, and it works for a good number of cases.

"If the same problems recur and a divorce is necessary, or the husband deserts the woman, we provide free legal aid," adds Dr Joshi.

In the last five years, 1,900 cases have come in to SNEHA. But that doesn't mean violence is increasing, it's just that it's getting *reported*.

Hanifabi adds, "*Kuch aadmi sudhar jaate hain, kuch waiseich rahenge.*"

But watch out, for the Superwomen of Dharavi are on the prowl.

"In our community, some people still think of marrying their daughters at 14-15 years of age," says Hanifabi.

But they don't actually dare to do it, because they know *khala* will march to the police station and complain.

Adds Salma, "*Auraton ko kamzor na samjho, hum mein bahut taakat hai.*"

It is this strength that helps Salma send her three daughters to English-medium schools, despite opposition from her husband.

"I want a better life for my girls. I don't want their dreams to be crushed like mine."

While her sixteen-year-old wants to become an air hostess, Salma prays her daughters find husbands who are educated and understanding.

Hanifabi is hopeful for the future.

"*Allah chahe to aagey aur achha hoga, ladkiyon ko aur izzat milegi.*"

Until then, more women will come forward to fight for themselves, and for others.

Ranis of Jhansi astride horses of valour. Charging through the narrow bylanes of the mind.

Which are as difficult to redevelop as Dharavi itself.

CHAPTER 19

MIND
THE
GAP

"What about girls who've dropped out of school?"

Dr Duru Shah's clinic is situated in fashionable Kemp's Corner. It's the kind of clinic where you find women in Gap maternity wear, debating on how to decorate the 'baby room'.

This is the Mumbai which believes it's already New York, if not yet Shanghai. And yet, these well-heeled patients are connected – in a small way – with their chappal-clad counterparts, in Dharavi.

The story goes back to the year 2000.

"I had two teenage daughters and I found their friends knew very little about their bodies, about periods and reproductive health," recalls Dr Shah.

Mothers don't talk about it; teachers skip 'that' chapter in the syllabus. So, where's a girl to turn?

As a gynaecologist, Dr Duru Shah felt *something* had to be done about this. In her capacity as President of FOGSI (Federation of Obstetric and Gynaecological Societies of India) she instituted a programme called 'Growing Up', in schools across Mumbai.

"The doctors prepared the master trainers and with the support of Johnson and Johnson, we extended the programme to seventy cities across India."

The 'Growing Up' programme educated girls from Class 5 to Class 8 on menstruation, nutrition, and contraception.

"The government tried to do the same things but failed, because they called it 'sex education', " observes Dr Shah.

While response to the programme was fantastic, one small thought bothered the good doctor: "What about girls who've dropped out of school?"

In fact, these are the girls who marry early, and get pregnant early. These are the girls who need information the most.

With this in mind, Duru met Dr Gurnani of UNICEF.

"This is a brilliant idea, we will support you!" he said.

He connected Duru with Dr Armida Fernandez, dean of Sion hospital, which is right next to Dharavi.

"Dr Fernandez offered us space at Chhota Sion Hospital, an extension of the main hospital."

Next, Dr Shah roped in ICDS (Integrated Child Development Service) or *anganwadi* workers, women who are the backbone of the community.

"This would help us reach out to girls through someone they know and trust."

But who would fund the programme?

"I was worrying about this when, one day, a patient who owns a big jewellery store started chatting with me," says Dr Shah.

The patient had been treated for fertility issues and was now expecting twins – she was on top of the world.

"I happened to mention the Dharavi project, and how we were struggling to raise money," recalls Dr Shah.

"How much do you need?" asked the patient.

Duru had no idea, but ₹ 25,000 a month sounded like a reasonable figure.

"I need ₹ 2.5 lakh," she replied.

The next morning, a cheque for ₹ 8 lakh was on Dr Shah's table. Now…it was all systems go!

The 'Kishori' project kicked off in the year 2001. The Department of Preventive & Social Medicine lent its support, while UNICEF provided the educational materials. A social worker was recruited to coordinate the activity and conduct sessions.

"We started with small things like getting blood tests done," says Dr Shah, "because anaemia is a huge problem with adolescent girls in India."

Health was a prime concern, but Kishori also addressed the issue of financial empowerment.

"I have always strongly felt that as a woman, you have to be on your feet, you have to earn," says Duru.

With this in mind, the Kishori project started offering classes in *mehendi*, hairdressing and tailoring. A patient donated four computers, and even promised to employ the girls after they were trained. But that's where the Kishori project stumbled.

"We found that there are very strong cultural stereotypes. Once a girl reaches puberty, she is not allowed to go outside the home and mohalla."

Even if they were picked up and dropped back by a company bus.

"We tried to talk to the parents, persuade them. But, we failed," admits Dr Shah.

Accepting ground realities, the Kishori project prodded on.

When Dr Shah delivered a lecture at Sophia College, she invited some of the students to volunteer at Kishori during their vacations.

"The Sophia girls came and taught our girls small things – how to say 'please' and 'thank you', how to lay a table, how to start a bank account."

The highlight of the Kishori project has been its 'annual day', when girls receive certificates and perform educational skits.

"We invited chief guests like Waheeda Rehman and Raveena Tandon. It was a great thrill for our girls," beams Dr Shah.

The biggest achievement of the Kishori project, however, has been the creation of 'peer educators' in the community.

"Girls go up to them and ask them questions on HIV, pregnancy or birth control, without hesitation," says Dr Shah.

Is the Kishori project a 'success'? What is the yardstick it should be judged by?

"As a doctor, I feel that if we focus on our adolescent girls today, they will be healthier and better mothers tomorrow," says Dr Shah.

And she believes the Kishori project can be a model for similar initiatives across the country.

"But right now, I am once again looking for space, looking for funding," she smiles.

Perhaps another happy patient will reach into her purse, and sign a cheque...

CHAPTER 20

BAREFOOT
RESEARCH

"The problems of the poor are similar across the world."

Babamma Deora is a girl who doesn't like to take 'tension' in life.

"Mujhe logon ke saath mil-jul kar rehna achha lagta hai…nayee nayee batein seekhana meri hobby hai."

One of the things Babamma learnt recently was how and why children work in the Dadar wholesale flowers market. That was the topic of the research project she undertook, as a 'youth fellow' with Pukar.

Babamma is merely 'tenth-standard pass' – not a PhD.

"I have done a para-professional course in social field," says the Dharavi girl, who works with Pratham, an NGO well-known for its work in education.

So what kind of research and what kind of fellowship is this anyway??

Welcome to Pukar (Partners for Urban Knowledge Research and Action), where curiosity is the only 'qualification' you need. This unusual organisation is an offshoot of the work of cultural anthropologist Arjun Appadurai.

"In 2004, Dr Appadurai wrote a seminal essay called 'Right to Research', " explains Dr Anita Patil-Deshmukh. "His idea was that research should not be restricted to scholars."

Even an ordinary man on the street can be a researcher, if given the chance. In fact, a paanwalla, or a young slum dweller, might capture a whole new body of knowledge. Hitherto ignored by scholars.

With this in mind, Dr Appadurai and his wife, historian Carol Breckenridge, decided to set up Pukar. A forum where ideas and people across disciplines, backgrounds and interests could come together.

"The 'Youth Fellowship Programme' is our flagship programme," explains Anita. "We believe the youth has a different way of looking at things. And that's why they can do great research."

You don't have to be from an elite college to apply for a fellowship. In fact, you could be a ragpicker, a fruit vendor or a school dropout.

"We train these young people and encourage them to pick subjects anchored in their own life-experience."

So, a group of Muslim girls choose to research why they must wear burkhas, while youngsters from Bainganwadi put together a poignant photo-essay on the water problem in their slum.

"We have trained four hundred youth over the last six years," beams Dr Anita. "At the heart of it, this is not just about creating knowledge, but also giving these young people life-skills."

Many Pukar youth fellows go on to work with NGOs, or start their own initiatives. Some also assist Pukar in its ongoing research project 'Mythologies of Mumbai', which documents the impact of globalisation on Girangaon and Dharavi.

"This is a Ford Foundation supported project, where we have spent three years following the lives of twenty-five families," adds Anita.

As well as GIS mapping of both communities.

Another project, supported by the Rockefeller Foundation, is looking at the mental health and social resilience of slum dwellers. A 'slum adversity' index, if you will.

"When you compare the data from slums with that of the National Family health survey, you find that the immunisation rate in slums is just 29%, as against 72% in the rest of the city!" exclaims Anita.

As a neonatologist working in inner city hospitals in the US for over twenty-five years, this is not exactly a shock for Dr Anita.

"The problems of the poor are similar across the world – lack of opportunity, lack of access," she observes.

It's just that in the US, 20% of the population is at the bottom of the pyramid, while in India it's 70%. And that is what attracted Dr Anita back to this country. To work from a municipal tenement in Kherwadi – the nerve centre of Pukar.

"Technically we are not situated *in* Dharavi, but everyone who wants to study Dharavi comes to Pukar," says Dr Anita.

Because knowledge does not need an academic greenhouse. It can bloom, anywhere.

CHAPTER 21

BREATHING EASY

"Most of our kids are
first-generation schoolgoers."

In Dharavi, an address is meaningless. Any place is only known by its
proximity to *another* place.

The Sri Sri Ravi Shankar Vidya Mandir School in Kalyanwadi is 'situated
behind the Ganesh mandir. A soft-spoken young volunteer guides us
through a maze of galis and gutters. Inside the compound wall is a
completely different world.

Fresh-faced, smartly dressed kids are doing PT in the tiny courtyard.
Classrooms are buzzing with activity. Soon it will be time for the
mid-day meal.

"We have 350 children in the school, which runs on two shifts," explains Meenakshi Sudhakar, full-time volunteer and vice-principal, SSRVM. "Five hundred kids are on the waiting list, but we just don't have space to expand further!"

It wasn't always like this.

"When Art of Living first came to Dharavi, people thought we wanted to convert them!"

The story begins in the year 2001, when Sri Sri Ravi Shankar visited Dharavi.

"Let us start some of our programmes here," he said to his young volunteers. *Magar kaise?* The Art of Living programme had spread from Malabar Hill to middle-class Mumbai, but had no experience in slums.

Two young professionals – Carl Avari and Zubin Pastakia – took up the challenge set up by Guruji.

"We dug out one contact in Vaibhav Cooperative Housing Society, a building which was part of the slum rehabilitation scheme in Dharavi," recalls Zubin.

The very first Art of Living satsang was held here, and slowly the word spread. The satsangs were about music and *masti,* but slowly started impacting minds.

"The residents of Vaibhav society got together and cleaned their paan-stained staircase!" says Zubin.

A Nav Chetna *shibir* was held, where participants learnt basics of health and hygiene, pranayama and meditation. Over the next few months, 2,000 Dharavi residents took the free course.

"The community was inspired to get together and convert a 4,000 sq ft dumping ground into a garden," says Zubin.

Some of the most enthusiastic participants in the Art of Living programmes were children, for whom special courses were held. But it soon became apparent to the volunteers that they lacked in one important life-skill: spoken English.

"We decided to start an informal English-medium school," says Carl.

The year was 2002. The 'school' operated from two rooms, each room further separated by an opaque curtain to create additional classrooms. There were no full-time teachers, only volunteers.

A hundred and seventy kids applied for just forty seats. By the end of the first year, it was clear that the Sri Sri Ravi Shankar Vidya Mandir Trust would have to expand. But where?

"We scouted all over Dharavi," recalls Carl. "It was hard, very hard work!"

After months of scrutiny, the team located some sheds in 'NDG compound', which was once a tannery.

"We felt these sheds could be converted into classrooms. But, of course, we would need to raise funds!"

Where there is a will, there is a way.

"And moreover, we always had Guruji's blessings," says Kedar Desai, another dedicated volunteer and co-founder of the school.

With support from patrons and corporate donors, pucca buildings, a science lab and tiled classrooms came into being. The school, as it stands today, was inaugurated in August 2007.

"At present we have ten rooms and run classes from nursery to Class 8," says Meenakshi. "We want to go right up to Class 12!"

Eighty per cent of the students cannot pay the fee of ₹ 250 per month – their education is sponsored by donors. But finance is not the only challenge.

"Most of our kids are first-generation schoolgoers," adds Meenakshi.

SSRVM is particular about its student-teacher ratio – there is one teacher for every twenty-five students. That's tough to maintain, given that the school has just thirty staff members, including admin.

"But somehow we manage," smiles Meenakshi.

The bigger issue is the exposure kids have to alcohol, drugs and violence in the home. The school, therefore, must work at a holistic level.

"All our students and teachers start the day with pranayama and meditation. This stabilises us all at a subtle level."

Malnourishment is another huge issue. SSRVM serves the students ragi cereal for breakfast and nutritious khichdi from the ISKCON kitchen at noon.

"We also have regular health camps and check-ups," adds Meenakshi. "And free tuitions are provided after school to the weak students."

Apart from all this, SSRVM runs a four-month hospitality-training programme for youth, in association with Westin Hotels. Skill-based education which improves employability of slum youth.

The bottom line is, there is a sense of change, a sense of hope.

"In the early days, many of the parents used to sell the textbooks we gave in *raddi*. Now, they attend PTA meetings and they have so many questions!"

And the Art of Living movement itself has touched over 30,000 residents of Dharavi.

"We have taught the *sudarshan kriya* in bylanes, small courtyards, cramped, unventilated rooms, amidst noise and stench!" adds Zubin.

People believe that the search for 'something deeper' is not relevant to those whose daily life is a struggle. But the Spirit exists in us all, and it longs to expand beyond limitations.

Whether a pauper or a prince, each of us must learn the 'art of living'.

With who we are, and what we have.

CHAPTER 22

YES
WE
CAN

POOR
LITTLE
RICH
SLUM

"That's one lesson she will
never forget."

The line is long and it moves slowly, but the children don't mind.
They shuffle past tables, all eyes and all ears.

On the other side are students of Chhatrapati Shivaji Vidyalaya, Sector 5,
Dharavi. Hosts of Agastya's Annual Science Fair.

Eleven-year-old Ayesha is explaining an exhibit on 'Seasons'.

"*Dekho yeh prithvi hai, yeh suraj*," she says, pointing out two globes.
She turns the earth on its axis expertly, to make her point.

By the time the three-day fair concludes, she would have explained the experiment hundreds of times.

"That's one lesson she will never forget," says Ramji Raghavan, whose vision to 'spark curiosity' in young minds led to the birth of Agastya, in 1999.

Ramji quit a high-flying career as a banker in London in the late 1990s, with a vague idea of 'doing something' in the field of education. Discussions with his father (former chairman of Engineers India) and a meeting with P K Iyengar, former chairman of the DAE (Department of Atomic Energy) set his path.

Dr Iyengar said, "Look Ram, this country can handle nuclear sanctions. Why? Because we have about 20,000 scientists who can develop whatever it needs."

That is the triumph of Indian science. The failure, however, is that the Nehruvian scientific temper never disseminated to the masses.

"Can you take up that challenge, Ramji?" asked Dr Iyengar.

And thus was born Agastya, a non-profit organisation whose mission was to make science 'fun' and accessible.

"We did not set out to create Ramanujans and C V Ramans or students who cracked IIT examinations," says Ramji. "The ideal was – and still is – to create a nation of 'problem-solvers'."

Ramji brainstormed for months on how to make this happen. And he arrived at a simple answer: creative people look at the ordinary and see something *more*. They observe, they assimilate and they apply.

"I remember a girl in Bangalore who said she did not remember a single thing she learnt in school or college – it was a waste of time. The only thing she recalled was a project where she built an African village."

Experiential learning is the key which opens the mind.

"We decided that Agastya would spark curiosity through very experiential, engaging learning."

'Seed capital' came in the form of a hundred low-cost science experiments, provided by the Homi Bhabha Centre for Science Education (HBSCE). The initial idea was to set up a science centre, for which Ramji acquired 172 acres of land near Kuppam, a small town in rural Andhra Pradesh.

"I had this vision of transforming a barren, rocky wasteland into lush forest."

But building this dream-campus was no joke. Very soon, Ramji ran out of money and the future became a question mark.

"So we thought, let the buildings get built when they get built. Let's take Agastya out there – *to* the people."

And thus, the Mobile Science Lab was born. A friend working at Hindustan Motors loaned the first vehicle. A tractor driver was trained as an instructor.

"He carried our low-cost experiments from village to village and it pulled crowds everywhere."

From this early success story came the idea of Mega Science Fairs, held over 2-3 days. Each fair attracts 10,000 to 15,000 students, and through them, Agastya reaches nearly one million children across eight states in India.

In 2009, for the first time, Agastya ventured into Mumbai. And it chose to hold this fair in Dharavi. The location is ideal – accessible from all over the city.

"It's an event our students look forward to all year," says Veena Donwalkar, principal of Chhatrapati Shivaji Vidyalaya. For, it is these children who are playing the role of 'instructor'.

Each child is assigned an experiment to explain at the fair. For many, the idea of speaking in public is terrifying, at first. By the end of the experience, they are transformed.

And in more ways than can be imagined.

"It turns out that you retain no more than 5% of what you hear in a lecture, 75% of what you personally experience, and over 90% of what you teach to others."

The point, however, is not that single experiment. It's an opening of the mind as a whole.

"I understand now that there is science in everything, all around us," says Gautam Thakur, a ninth standard Hindi-medium student who lives in Dharavi.

"What do you mean?" probes Ramji.

"Well, I mean look at the fan, look at this chair – none of it would be possible without science," replies the boy.

Maybe this boy goes to college, maybe he doesn't. But in some small way, this fair has changed his attitude to life. And that will stay with him.

"I want to take some kids from Dharavi to our Kuppam campus," adds Ramji. "I want to expose them not just to science, but to the beauty of nature."

It is this exposure to nature which rural children have used to their advantage.

For four years in a row, children from Agastya's Young Instructor Leader programme have been winning the IRIS Intel National Science Fair. And most of their ideas for projects come from the world around them – insects, animals, trees.

"Two village girls who can't speak English are going to America this year, to demonstrate their project," beams Ramji.

Beating rich kids with everything money can buy.

A seed has been planted in Dharavi.
One day, it could be a mighty tree.

POOR
LITTLE
RICH
SLUM

SECTION 4

THE FUTURE

*Where do we go from here –
forward or backward? You talk
about development but, pray tell
me, when will it happen?*

CHAPTER 23

CIRCLE
OF
LIFE

POOR
LITTLE
RICH
SLUM

"... Ab kaun jhanjhat mein
padega?"

Skin head dead head
Everybody gone bad
Situation, aggravation
Everybody allegation...

All I wanna say is that
They don't really care about us.

– Michael Jackson
They Don't Really Care About Us

Krishna Prajapati* is a thin, short, dour, angry old man.

He has spent sixty-nine years of his life, bent over the pottery wheel, like his father and his grandfather before him.

But, *aage kya hoga, kuch nahin pata.*

"My father left our ancestral village in Saurashtra in 1933 and came to Dharavi. I was born here in Kumbharwada."

Kumbharwada – or potter's colony – is one of the oldest settlements in Dharavi. They came to escape drought and famine. And found the wide open landscape of Dharavi most suitable for their traditional form of work.

"Originally we *kumbhars* could get plenty of *matti* from Dharavi itself."

The soil in Dharavi was, however, black. Hence the kumbhars also procured mud from Kalina (an area five kilometres away) and sieved the two mattis together.

"In those days (1950s), we were the main residents here, apart from Kolis (fishermen)."

Standing in Kumbharwada, it was possible to see Mahim Station on one side and the trains passing on the central line.

"There were no *jhopad pattis* back then."

Things slowly started changing in the 1960s. Kumbharwada, once an exclusive potters' colony, started having 'mixed' residents.

"There was demand for rooms on rent. So some people started making extra rooms and taking tenants."

Meanwhile, the world itself was changing. The next generation of kumbhars, who went to school and some even to college, did not want to continue with their traditional business.

"*Padhne-likhne ke baad koi matti mein haath nahin dalna chahta hai!*" exclaims Prajapati.

Knowledge, which is not passed down from one generation to the next, slowly dies.

Business, which is not passed down from one generation to the next, slowly withers.

The kumbhars continue making pots just like they did one hundred years ago. Prajapati is dimly aware that there is better technology – mechanised wheels and *gas ki bhatti*. But *dhandha chal raha hai*, there is no hurry to make the change.

There are many new opportunities in the market. New kinds of pots and diyas are in demand.

"People from outside come and buy our pots, they paint them, add glitter and sell them in big shops."

A diya bought in Kumbharwada for ₹ 10 can sell for ₹ 100 at fancy department stores, cellophane-wrapped.

So why don't the kumbhars upgrade themselves and directly supply to the stores?

"Some people do it…but you see, only one of my sons is helping me in business…" he trails off.

Prajapati is too old, too tired. Resigned to life as he has seen it for sixty-nine years. *Ab kaun jhanjhat mein padega?*

"I do my work, *kharcha-pani nikal jata hai*. I have no desires beyond that."

The kumbhars are fighting a losing battle, to preserve their way of life.

"We do not wish to be part of Dharavi Redevelopment Plan (DRP). We want self-development."

The kumbhars want not only homes but space for their wheels and kilns. And open areas to dry their pots in the sun. Provisions which do not exist in the current plan.

"We are willing to get together and invest money, to make our plan a reality. We don't want to live in a *kabutarkhana* just because the government is giving it free of cost."

That may just be empty rhetoric. Because in another twenty years, the wheels which silently shaped the formless clay, may well stop turning. Kumbharwada will be just another meaningless name like Bainganwadi, where baingans or brinjals once grew.

Is there a place for kumbhars in a city which prefers Tupperware containers over *matkas*?

No kumbhars, no baingans. Tupperware City wants only numbered high-rise apartment blocks.

* *Name changed on request*

POOR
LITTLE
RICH
SLUM

> " Nowadays people are taking multiple electricity bills for the same kholi so they can grab more than one room when there is redevelopment. "
>
> – Anand Kumar*
> Jewellery shop owner, Sakinabai Chawl

* Name changed on request

CHAPTER 24

FUTURE
SHOCK

POOR
LITTLE
RICH
SLUM

"Complete redevelopment of Dharavi is the endeavour of DRP."

Space, the final frontier.

These are the promises of Dharavi redevelopment.

Pass the 3-D glasses and a tub of buttered popcorn.

Let us take you on a walk through Dharavi 2.0, or, Dharavi after DRP.

We start with an aerial shot of the vast, corrugated tin-roofed landscape, as it stands today.

Tight close-ups of old buildings.

Dirty nullahs and tight galis.

No drinking water.

Mountains of filth.

Pollution, sanitation.

The camera lingers on these images, like the 'before' version of a pimply teen model. Waiting for her makeover into My Fair Lady.

Dharavi nagri ki sarvangi vikas hai DRP ki koshish. (Complete redevelopment of Dharavi is the endeavour of DRP.)

Dharavi ki rehvasaiyon ka aur udyogon ka suniyojit punarvasan kiya jayege. (We will resettle both industry and residents in a planned manner.)

There will be a 'transparent tender process'.

Aapko sehbhagi banakar apke muddon ko nazar rakhte hi prakalp ka prayojan kiya jayega. (We will invite you to participate in this process and keep in mind your issues.)

That was the trailer, now comes the main film. An artist's vision of Dharavi – as it *will* be.

Neat and attractive pastel-coloured buildings, on two-storey high 'podiums'.

The podiums are for shops, business and industrial activity. And connected to each other by 'green skywalks'.

Every shop will be 14 ft high. Each building, 12 m apart. Ample light, good ventilation.

Even a basement car park!

Every building will have its own playground. Every area, its own gyms, hospitals, post offices and police stations.

Six per cent of the area will be a 'community space', reserved for home business.

You see, we have thought of *everything*.

Now, here's the 'sample flat'.

Each house measures 300 sq ft.

This is the living room – velvet sofa, flat-screen TV and modern art on the wall. Come, see the modular kitchen, isn't it nice?

Here is your bedroom, with a built-in cupboard. Do you like the bedspread?

Come, see your study room with computer (LCD monitor).

Itna sab kuch 300 sq ft mein?

This is a work of science fiction.

The fiction of making promises.

The science of never keeping them.

The ten-year-old mission of the Dharavi Redevelopment Project.

To boldly go where no slum has gone before!

Currently, still in the process of inviting tenders.
Currently, still in the process of conducting surveys.
Currently, still in the process of painting dreams.

While another generation grows up in filth and darkness.

The 3-D Walk-Through *is a CD, prepared and distributed by the Dharavi Redevelopment Project.*

Disclaimer on cover of CD: "This plan is for the purpose of information only."

POOR
LITTLE
RICH
SLUM

CHAPTER 25

WAITING
FOR
GODOT

POOR
LITTLE
RICH
SLUM

"The government has no political will."

Raju Korde was born in Dharavi.
He has grown up in Dharavi.
He still lives in Dharavi.

"*Yahan ke redevelopment ki jo kahani hai wo mere jitni lambi hai*," says the lawyer and social activist.

And the man is forty-three years old.

The Dharavi of Raju's childhood consisted of huts made of jute and *khalli*. A brick house or a house with a tin roof was a luxury.

"There was no running water, no public toilet, no street, no streetlight."

Dharavi was a 'slum' in the truest sense of the word. An illegal occupation which was not entitled to any amenities from the government.

In the year 1971, the Maharashtra Slum Areas (Improvement, Clearance and Redevelopment) Act came into being.

"*Yeh ek krantikari kanoon tha*," says Raju. Because for the first time, the State acknowledged that slum dwellers have some 'rights'.

While the intention of the Act was to 'make better provisions for the improvement and clearance of slum areas and their redevelopment', the actual message it gave was very simple.

"*Jo jahan rehta hai, woh ghar uska ho gaya.*"

Not much redevelopment actually took place over the next twenty years. In fact, in 1973, a 'Slum Improvement Board' was constituted. This brought basic civic amenities to Dharavi – taps, drainage, pathways, latrines and streetlights.

Still, the living conditions were so pathetic that when the then Prime Minister Rajiv Gandhi visited Dharavi in 1986, he was shaken enough to sanction ₹ 100 crore for the area's development.

But his own party workers protested, "This is not the only slum!"

Thus, of the sanctioned ₹ 100 crore, only ₹ 37 crore actually went to Dharavi. Of this approximately ₹ 22 crore went towards infrastructure development. In particular, the main artery of Dharavi, fondly known as the '90-ft Road'.

The remaining ₹ 15 crore was used for housing projects. But given the size and scale of the township, this was just a symbolic redevelopment.

An ant crawling on the leg of an elephant.

In 1995, the SRA (Slum Rehabilitation Authority) came into being. And the idea of a 'free house' became a reality. To those with proof of residence in Mumbai, before 1 January 1995.

"All these buildings you see in Dharavi on Link Road and 90-ft Road, are because of the SRA scheme," says Raju.

Under the SRA scheme, private builders could redevelop a slum, with the consent of seventy per cent of its residents. These developers would provide a 225 sq ft home, free of cost to the slum dweller, but in return receive commercially valuable TDR* (transferable development rights).

"In Dharavi, the builder gets 1.33 units for sale for every 1 unit constructed free of cost. That's more attractive than in the city or suburbs."

Which is why so many builders made a beeline for Dharavi. Creating four-storey buildings of peeling paint. Which look only marginally less slum-like than the slum itself.

In 2004, the government decided to stop individual SRA projects in Dharavi. Instead, the whole area would be redeveloped – according to a Master Plan.

A dream which, eight years later, lies locked in a CD. A mirage, unseen and unimplemented on the ground.

"Government mein political will hi nahin hai."

And the 'Dharavi Bachao Andolan' or 'Save Dharavi Movement' started by residents like Raju Korde has been another factor.

Between 2002 and 2010, he published a newspaper called *Dharavi Times* – in Hindi, Marathi and Urdu. With the objective of *'jan jaagran'*.

"We are not against development," he clarifies. "*But yahan kis ka development ho raha hai – insaan ka ya zameen ka?*"

The fact is the land is what makes development attractive to both the State and the commercial community. Are the people who inhabit it equally important?

The Dharavi Bachao Andolan believes it is not so.

"There is no transparency and no understanding of what the people really need, or want."

In these seven years, the government has made some concessions. The size of free tenements has been increased from 225 sq ft to 300 sq ft. And the cut-off date for eligibility from 1995 to 2000.

"But that will not solve the basic problem," says Raju. "Dharavi has a floating population, buy *aur* sale *chalta rehta hai*."

Fifty per cent of the current residents are not eligible for a free home, or alternate accommodation. Because they are living on rent, or have bought a kholi after the year 2000.

"If you buy a house in Dadar or Andheri or Cuffe Parade, do you need to be on the electoral roll since the year 2000? Why are rules for the poor always different?" he counters.

The Dharavi Bachao Andolan has a simple solution: redevelop structure for structure. That takes into account rights of tenants, landlords, *and* all those who bought huts on pagdi basis.

To say with pride, "I have a home in Mumbai."

Committees meet, announcements are made. Meanwhile, life goes on.

"The way water flows in the river, even human beings always flow towards development," says Raju philosophically.

"Magar swarg mein bhi lekar jao to razamandi chahiye…"

Dharavi is no paradise soon to be lost. But to those who reign there, it is a hell worth fighting for.

*TDR can be used to construct additional housing or commercial units for sale in the free market. Or, these rights can be sold to other builders.

CHAPTER 26

DAVID
VS
GOLIATH

"Why can't a million people
make up an SEZ?"

The School of Planning and Architecture is to a young architect, what IIM is to a young manager. An institution with a pedigree which opens many doors.

With a Master's from SPA, Aneerudha Paul could easily be working for The Firm. Designing golf courses and penthouse apartments in Gurgaon and New Cuffe Parade.

Instead, he occupies a spartan office in suburban Mumbai and works as the director of Kamla Raheja Vidyanidhi Institute of Architecture and Environmental Studies (KRVIA). And, he fights for a city as it can be. As it should be, to take its rightful place in the world.

"I joined KRVIA in 1993 and worked extensively with the research and design cell at the institute. We took up select work which allowed us to critically look at architecture."

The first project Aneerudha worked on was to do with redevelopment of mill lands. Along with the Charles Correa committee, KRVIA prepared a report on how mill land could be made use of in a way which would benefit the city, and not just a few private builders. But, that is exactly what happened.

"Ultimately, no space was released for public amenities, neither did any low-cost housing get built."

Another project KRVIA worked on was the Eastern Waterfront, a vast tract of land in the eastern part of Mumbai which is not being optimally used. The researchers concluded that if this land was properly released, it could give back to Mumbai much-needed public space.

A book documenting the Eastern Waterfront and its potential was released by KRVIA, in collaboration with UDRI (Urban Design Research Institute).

"Of course, nothing has come out of our recommendations..." admits Aneerudha.

And yet, his idealism remained unchanged. When the Dharavi Redevelopment Plan was announced, a group of concerned citizens including architects, planners, academicians and activists questioned the format of the project. Aneerudha Paul was one of them.

"The plan was simply to give five sectors to five builders for redevelopment. There was no understanding, no framework, no survey work conducted."

Negotiations with the state government took place, but they refused to yield, on any ground. So the group wrote to the prime minister, pointing out that this was not a greenfield project – a piece of land which can be divided and handed over.

"In fact, we suggested that Dharavi should be seen as an SEZ – a Special Economic Zone. Why can't a million people make up an SEZ rather than just a few conglomerates?"

Seen through such a lens, the entire project takes on a different, more democratic character.

"What we saw was a lot of lip service for the poor, but an intention to free up costly land and hand it over to private builders."

'Rehabilitation' in fifty-storey buildings was another part of the redevelopment plan which the group vehemently opposed. On both practical and moral grounds.

"It is proven historically that high-rise buildings do not work for low-income people," says Aneerudha.

So, what is the alternative? asked the government.

To look into that, an advisory committee was formed in 2007, with representation for activists and technical experts like Aneerudha. A positive outcome of these efforts was that the government finally agreed to commission a survey of Dharavi through the NGO, Mashaal.

"We were also asked to look at one small sector – Sector 4 – and give an alternate plan for development," adds Aneerudha.

The R & D cell of Kamla Raheja Institute conducted its own survey of Sector 4, documenting the entire informal systems around which Dharavi is organised. This includes the *nagars*, chawls, housing societies and industrial compounds.

"The government map looks like this," says Aneerudha pointing to five big blocks marked Sectors 1, 2, 3, 4 and 5. "Our map looks like this!"

Dozens of small pockets, marked in different colours to denote their unique character.

"If you see Dharavi as a collection of small pockets, each pocket can then be developed according to the need of its residents."

For example, Kumbharwada, or the colony of potters, is a work-based nagar. So it cannot be redeveloped merely as an apartment complex, it must have an industrial-cum-residential character.

"We are not against a master plan," clarifies Aneerudha. "But the plan need not have straight lines. An organic pattern already exists, we can work with that."

Any nagar or chawl must be redeveloped with the full knowledge and participation of its residents. Otherwise, there is bound to be resistance and opposition.

What's more, Aneerudha firmly believes that the initial plan should not involve builders at all.

"Some communities have money, they are willing to bear the construction cost. Others may say, we want a builder to come in – then we demarcate a pocket for the builder."

Some land would have to be vacated by existing residents, to hand over. But since the community has been taken into confidence, they will do so willingly.

"The government can invite builders to bid for the vacated plots and the money thus raised can be used to build 'free' housing in that pocket?" adds Aneerudha.

The beauty of this strategy is that the builder gets a 'greenfield project' – an area free of dispute. And the community gets a larger portion of land for common use and benefit.

"The project becomes financially viable if the builder is given just twenty-one per cent of the land," says Aneerudha.

Whereas in the Master Plan, as it stands today, builders will take over seventy-five per cent of Dharavi. Clearly, other forces are at work here.

"The problem is that builders see 'redevelopment' merely as a means to make money. But cities are so much more than that!"

And that is what experts like Aneerudha are asking us to think about.

Are we redesigning our cities to merely *look* good. Or do we wish to *do* good?

"The vision for our city must be inclusive," believes Aneerudha. "Otherwise 'development' will lead to chaos."

Does Dharavi need harsh, invasive surgery? Or does it need slow and gentle rehabilitation, one dysfunctional part at a time?

While we dilly-dally indefinitely, the soul keeps a gasping body alive…

> *Right now, only the owner of the structure is eligible for alternate housing. What will happen to the rest – who form the majority? Nobody knows where they will go… after all, we have no concept of 'low-income housing' apart from slums, in this city.*
>
> – Aneerudha Paul
> Director, Kamla Raheja School of Architecture

CHAPTER 27

GENERATION NEXT

"I am not ashamed of my
background, but..."

Syed Gani is an assistant manager at California Pizza Kitchen. An
upscale eatery in upscale BKC, the financial district whose towers can be
seen from any rooftop in Dharavi.

Syed is just twenty-two. In the three years since completing his BSc in
'Catering and Hospitality Administration', he's risen quickly. From trainee
to captain, to his current position. But it is not enough.

"I want to go abroad, work abroad... I will go to Europe or Canada,
or Singapore. I want to earn a lot of money, come back and start
a restaurant!"

Nothing unusual about Syed's ambition. With an education, with experience, with energy and enthusiasm – a young man like him may well make it from Mahim to Manhattan.

But, what if he is not actually from Mahim?

"The moment I write 'Dharavi' and apply for a job, I will be rejected," he says matter of factly. "I always put my address as Mahim East."

Syed is born and brought up in Dharavi. His father and grandfather and great-grandfather have lived in Dharavi.

"I am not ashamed of my background. I grew up here, all my friends are here."

And yet. He must downplay this background, deny his roots. To be 'accepted' in the outside world.

'The image of Dharavi is very poor," he shrugs. "It's a slum area."

Within this slum, there are pockets of affluence. The house Syed calls 'home' is not typical of Dharavi.

"It's a big area, proper construction. We have an attached toilet, washing machine, Dish TV, fridge – everything."

Everything but respect. When Syed went to the bank for an education loan, he was turned down.

"I gave a guarantee, even my house as a security, but I could not get the loan."

Ultimately, the family shelled out ₹ 4 lakh for Syed's hotel management course. Which makes him all the more determined to go abroad, and 'recover' the amount quickly.

Not everyone is as lucky.

"Most of the students pass Class 10 and join degree courses. Science, or Commerce or Arts (only for girls)."

A degree course costs very little – ₹ 6,000 to ₹ 7,000 per annum, while a professional course can go into lakhs.

"Also there is no one to guide the students here in Dharavi. They don't know about BMS (Bachelor in Management Studies), they don't know about CAT."

There is no 'Super 30' in Dharavi, inspiring students to dream of getting into an IIT. Saboo Siddik, an engineering college in Mumbai run by the Anjuman-i-Islam trust, is a more popular choice.

Syed of Mahim East wants to see the world.
Syed of Dharavi promises he will return.
But, will he return *to* Dharavi?

"I will come back, then let's see. It depends on my mom and dad also... I have a responsibility towards them."

He looks uncertain.

"I will never leave Mumbai...that's for sure," he says.

Will 'Dharavi' ever be just another part of Mumbai? Or will young men like Syed always have to make a choice?

Between roots and respectability.

Between reality and practicality.

How long will opportunity be denied to young men like Syed, just due to the accident of an address?

CHAPTER 28

FINAL THOUGHTS

*A Big, Fat Problem
or
A Big, Fat Solution?*

POOR
LITTLE
RICH
SLUM

> "Economies are not built
> on capital alone."

Success stories are usually about individuals. Those wise and centred beings who make it, despite all odds.

In doing so, they guide us, inspire us, push us to reach somewhere deep within. And create the world we want, for ourselves.

Dharavi is the success story of a community. A million individuals who have come together to create their own unique brand.

You and I may be born in Mumbai, but *where* we live is merely a transit point. Do we really think twice before moving to a bigger apartment, a different city or even a different country?

We are tigers in the urban jungle, solitary and self-sufficient.

If you are born in Dharavi, it's different. The web of human relationships envelops you, supports you, nourishes you.

"*Hum log cement ke ghar mein nahin, insaaniyat ke ghar mein rehte hain,*" proclaimed one gentleman we met.

Filmi as it sounds, there is no better way to put it.

Dharavi is not just a physical location, it is an emotional entity. A city within a city, with the soul of a village.

Economies are not built on capital alone. They are the products of human intent. Dharavi is what you get when a million people hold a common intention. To rise above their circumstances, and make the best life possible for themselves.

When a trainee joins a company, he observes 'how things happen'. Quickly, he learns to walk the talk, to fit in.

It's the same with Dharavi. Every new immigrant is sucked into the can-do culture of this special economic zone.

There is no founder, no CEO, but this *is* an entrepreneurial organisation. Where each works independently yet depends on the other. And therefore, owes allegiance to the whole.

Dharavi should be celebrated and replicated.

Because every human being has the potential to be ignited.

Poverty is nothing but a state of mind.

THE
ELEPHANT
IN THE
ROOM

POOR
LITTLE
RICH
SLUM

It was six men of Indostan
To learning much inclined,
Who went to see the Elephant
(Though all of them were blind)

Lo and behold the Elephant
They see it whole and wide
Its majesty is evident
It is a source of pride

Alas the greed of man prevails
They care not for the whole
They want its precious ivory
That is the only goal

No matter if the elephant
Is wounded or is maimed
Now if that elephant goes rogue
You know who must be blamed...

DHARAVI RESOURCE LIST

If you would like to contact any of the amazing individuals –
entrepreneurs, thinkers and believers – featured in this book, here they
are (in order of appearance):

Be The Local Tours: info@bethelocaltoursandtravels.com;
www.bethelocaltoursandtravels.com

Srini Swaminathan: srini@teachforindia.org; www.teachforindia.org

Jameel Shah, Shah Shoes: shahshoes@yahoo.in
Shah Shoes is also on Facebook

Mohammed Mustaqeem: azimcmcraft@gmail.com

Ayyappa Idli Stall: Opp Shankara Mattam temple, Telang Rd, Matunga (E)

Mushtaq Syed: INMA entreprises: inmaent@bom4.vsnl.net.in;
www.inmaenterprises.com

Rani Nadar: c/o rebecca.nadar@yahoo.in

Waterwalla: info@waterwalla.org; www.waterwalla.org

Jockin Arputham: sparcnsdfmm@gmail.com; www.sparcindia.org

Dr Jalindar Adsule: jadsule@gmail.com

Walter Fischer, Barefoot Acupuncture : walter.apn@gmail.com

Ujwala Patil: patil.uju@gmail.com; www.barefootacupuncturists.com

Vinod Shetty, Acorn Foundation: dharaviproject@gmail.com;
www.dharaviproject.org

Praveen Sakpal: Gurudutt Gymnasium, Sion-Koliwada, Dharavi

SNEHA: snehamumbai@snehamumbai.org; www.snehamumbai.org

Dr Duru Shah: durushah@hotmail.com

PUKAR: pukar@pukar.org.in; www.pukar.org.in

Art of Living School: ssrvmdharavi@gmail.com; www.dharavischool.org

Agastya Foundation: agastyaadmin@gmail.com; www.agastyafoundation.org

Dharavi Redevelopment Project: http://www.sra.gov.in/htmlpages/dharavi.htm

Aneerudha Paul: info@krvia.ac.in; www.krvia.ac.in

Manik Prabhavati, Daya Sadan Community Centre: manikprabhavati@gmail.com; http://www.karmayog.org/ngo/daya

Adolf Tragler, Slum Rehabilitation Society: atragler@gmail.com; www.srsindia.org

Raju Korde: advrdkorde@gmail.com

POOR
LITTLE
RICH
SLUM

Brahmanand Swaroopa Isha Jagadisha

**Because everything is an image of
the ecstasy of the Creator**

ACKNOWLEDGEMENTS

A heartfelt 'thank you' to the many wonderful people who helped us in researching and writing this book.

Fahim Vora and Tauseef Siddiqui, for sharing their lives and connecting us with their community, as only insiders can.

Dr Farida Lambay and Dr Jalindar Adsule of Nirmala Niketan College of Social Work. Thank you for sharing your perspectives and the use of the college library for our work.

Dr Wasundhara Joshi and her team at SNEHA – in particular, Jenny – for arranging numerous valuable interviews.

Ms Geeta Verghese, Mr M R Khan and Mr Ashok Khaire of the State Bank of India, for generously sharing information on urban microfinance.

To Venkat Krishnan, for his encouragement and his introductions.

And to Sunil Handa, for being an early sceptic (it only made us more determined, to put heart and soul into this book).

Our deep gratitude to Abhijit Bansod and his team at Studio ABD, for designing this book. Because they are as fascinated by Dharavi as we are.

To Saurabh Datar, for the exacting job of proofreading.

Thank you to Westland – to Gautam Padmanabhan, Paul Vinay Kumar and Aradhana Bisht – for believing in us, and our vision for the book.

To driver Reddy, who ferried us from Sion to Matunga and everywhere in between.

And Café Mysore, whose masala dosas and filter coffees gave us the energy to go back again and again. To see 'what more?'.

To all those who welcomed us into their homes and hearts.

Who made us feel a part of their lives, for a few brief moments.

Moments we will treasure and carry within, wherever we go.

Also by Rashmi Bansal

From the author of the bestsellers
Stay Hungry Stay Foolish & Connect the Dots

I have a
Dream

RASHMI BANSAL

The inspiring stories of
20 social entrepreneurs who found new ways
to solve old problems

Sold over 100,000 copies

The inspiring stories of 25 IIM
Ahmedabad graduates who chose
to tread a path of their own making

STAY HUNGRY STAY FOOLISH

Rashmi Bansal

Sold over 300,000 copies

From the author of the bestseller
STAY HUNGRY STAY FOOLISH

Rashmi Bansal

CONNECT THE D•TS

The inspiring stories of
20 entrepreneurs without an MBA
who dared to find their own path

Sold over 150,000 copies